Newspaper Indexes:

A Location and Subject Guide

for Researchers

Volume II

by

ANITA CHEEK MILNER

The Scarecrow Press, Inc.
Metuchen, N.J., & London
1979

Library of Congress Cataloging in Publication Data   (Revised)

Milner, Anita Cheek.
  Newspaper indexes.

   1. American newspapers--Indexes--Bibliography--
Union lists. 2. Newspapers--Indexes--Bibliography--
Union lists. 3. Catalogs, Union--United States.
I. Title.
Z6951.M635   016.071   77-7130
ISBN 0-8108-1244-4

For

APRIL MAURINE SABENS MILNER

CONTENTS

INTRODUCTION

The bulk of this work was included in a thesis presented to the faculty of San Diego State University in spring, 1978, in partial fulfillment of the requirements for the degree of Master of Arts in Special Education, with Emphasis on the Gifted.

To gather information for this volume 995 questionnaires were mailed to libraries, newpapers, historical and genealogical societies, and selected individuals. The questions asked were, in essence, the same as those asked for Volume I* of this title:

What newspaper indexes do you have and for what years?

What subjects are covered in the indexes?

What is the charge for having a staff member check the index for a requested reference?

What is the cost of a photocopy of an article?

Are newspapers available on interlibrary loan?

Is there a catalog or other publication available? What is the price?

Arrangement of This Book

There were 266 returned questionnaires that provided information on newspaper indexes. The responses have been arranged in two main sections. In the first half of the book, news-

---

*Milner, Anita Cheek. *Newspaper Indexes: A Location and Subject Guide for Researchers.* Scarecrow Press, 1977.

papers are listed by name under their subjects of interest or the county and state of publication, giving the years indexed and the Library of Congress symbol for each repository. This Library of Congress symbol is the key to the second half of the work. Under the corresponding symbols in this section are listed the answers to the other six questions that were asked. Correct addresses are given, the type of subjects indexed, and information relative to having the index checked and articles photocopied, as well as the accessibility of the newspaper through Interlibrary Loan.

* * * *

The compiler makes no claims for the accuracy of the information in this book. Answers were transcribed from returned questionnaires as accurately as possible, with a minimum of revision.

Information and prices quoted are, generally, valid for the latter half of 1977. All prices and policies are subject to change at any time.

Additions and corrections are invited for a subsequent volume. Write: Mrs. Anita Cheek Milner, 1511 Rincon Villa Drive, Escondido, CA 92027.

Acknowledgments

It would be impossible to repay the encouragement, help, and time given me by my thesis committee; Dr. Leif Fearn (Chair), Dr. Robert McCabe, and Dr. Daniel Weinberg. My thanks to all three of you.

A.C.M.

KEY

Ca. Around

+ Newspapers are indexed to the present; an ongoing project.

I Fee for checking the index for a reference.

C Fee for making a photocopy of a specific article. Price given is for each sheet of paper needed to photocopy a cited article. Some articles will take more than one sheet of paper. Unless otherwise stated, prices refer to 8½″ × 11″ sheets of paper.

ILL Newspapers are available on Interlibrary Loan. Almost without exception the newspapers will be on microfilm. "Hard copy" refers to the original newspaper.

* Designates libraries, societies or individuals that have not been given symbols in the 11th edition of the Library of Congress' *Symbols of American Libraries*. The compiler used the guidelines in that book to assign symbols.

** Indexes for newspapers preceded by this symbol may be found in many of the larger public or university libraries. Dates held will vary.

SASE Self-addressed stamped envelope.

AMERICAN FOREIGN LANGUAGE NEWSPAPERS

CARPATHO-RUTHENIAN

Amerikansky Russky Viestnik (Homestead, PA)	1894–1914	MnU-IA

GERMAN

La Crosse, WI newspaper	Ca. 1853–Early 1900's	WLac

CHURCH PUBLICATIONS

BAPTIST

Religious Herald (State paper of Virginia Baptists)	1828–1873	ViRVB

JEWISH

American and Western Hemisphere Jewish newspapers	No dates given	OCAJA
Asmonean, Occident, Israelite (American Israelist), Jewish Messenger, Sinai, Zeitgeist	19th century	MWalA

DENOMINATIONAL INDEXING

AMISH AND MENNONITES

Intelligencer Journal (Lancaster, PA)	1900–1960 Ca. 1960 +	PLMHi PLMHi
New Era (Lancaster, PA)	Ca. 1970 +	PLMHi
Sunday News (Lancaster, PA)	Ca. 1972 +	PLMHi

METHODIST

Various newspapers	No dates given	TNMPH

PRESBYTERIAN AND REFORMED CHURCHES

Asheville (NC) Times (And other national and international newspapers and periodicals)	1965 +	NcMHi

SCHWENKFELDER

(Sumneytown) *Bauern Freund* (Montgomery County, PA)	1830–1861	PPeSchw

SHAKERS

Miscellaneous newspapers	1880's +	NOcaS

SWEDENBORGIAN

Miscellaneous newspapers	1800 +	MNtS

SPECIALIZED SUBJECTS

CANALS

Syracuse (NY) Herald Journal	1962 +	NSyCM
Syracuse (NY) Post Standard	1962 +	NSyCM

HERBERT HOOVER

Miscellaneous newspapers	1917–1964	IaWbH
	1933–1964	IaWbH

RAILROADS

New York Times, Chicago Tribune, Washington Post, Washington Star, New York Journal of Commerce, Wall Street Journal	Ca. 1962 +	DBRE

SOUTHWESTERN UNITED STATES

Durango Herald	1972 +	CoDuF

THEATER

New York newspapers	1900–1970	PPFR
Philadelphia newspapers	1900–1970	PPFR

WOMEN

Miscellaneous newspapers	No dates given	DAAUW

INDIVIDUAL STATES

ALABAMA

Calhoun County

Anniston Star	1900 +	AAnn

Cherokee County

The (Centre) Cherokee Advertiser	1866–1887	ACeSU
The (Centre) Cherokee Sentinel	1890–1897	ACeSU
The (Centre) Coosa River News	1880–1901	ACeSU

Dallas County

The Selma Daily Messenger	9 September 1867; 26 February 1974	AMobM

Jefferson County

Birmingham News	1950–1962	AU
Birmingham News Magazine (Sunday supplement)	1950–1962	AU

Lee County

Auburn Bulletin	No dates given	ALoaLHi
Opelika-Auburn News	No dates given	ALoaLHi

Limestone County

   Athens News Courier   August 1976   ADeW

Mobile County

   Mobile newspapers   1822 +   AMobHI

   Ballou's Pictorial Drawingroom Com- 27 June 1857   AMobM
     panion

   The Blakeley Sun and Alabama Adver- 6 April 1819   AMobM
     tiser

   Citronelle Times   2 January 1897   AMobM

   (Fort Morgan) *Home Ties*   May 1919   AMobM

   Grand Bay News   29 October 1915   AMobM

   The (Grand Bay) Times-News   12 October 1921   AMobM

   Mobile Advertiser and Register   2 March 1862;
                                       24 March 1863   AMobM

   (Mobile) *Alabama Staats-Zeitung*   3 January 1901   AMobM

   (Mobile) *Barton News*   November 1922   AMobM

   (Mobile) *Brookley Spotlight* (Air Force 23 June 1963   AMobM
     Base)

   The (Mobile) Carnival Record   26 February 1889   AMobM

   Mobile Commercial Register   November 1823;
                                       1 August 1826   AMobM

   Mobile Commercial Register and   26 April 1834;
     Patriot   2 August 1839   AMobM

   Mobile Daily Advertiser and Chronicle 1 January 1842   AMobM

   Mobile Daily Herald   29 December 1897;
                                       2 January 1898; 18
                                       May 1902; 11 Feb-
                                       ruary 1960   AMobM

The Mobile Daily Item	9 May 1898; 15, 19 September 1901; 24 February 1903; 8 February 1904; 26 April 1910; 21 July 1912; 2 August 1914; February, July, August 1918 (Bound and for full month)	AMobM
The Mobile Daily News	15, 16 April, 25, 27, 28 May 1865; 20 December 1893	AMobM
Mobile Daily Tribune	19 December 1869	AMobM
The Mobile Democrat	7 October 1928	AMobM
The (Mobile) Fairy	2, 5 January 1875	AMobM
The (Mobile) Gulf Coast Farmer	February 1939	AMobM
The (Mobile) Gypsie	31 December 1877; 1 January 1878	AMobM
(Mobile) *Life Assurance Gazette*	November 1868	AMobM
(Mobile) *Merchants and Planters Price Current*	17 April 1841; 8 January, 26 February 1842	AMobM
(Mobile) *Murphy Hi Times*	20 March, 8 May 1936; 5 March 1938; 11 September, 9, 23 October, 6 November, 4 December 1940; 27 January, 5, 19 December 1941; 11 April 1, 22 May 1942; 19 January, 24 November 1943; 1, 10 March 1944	AMobM
The (Mobile) Musical Courier	24 June 1908	AMobM

The (Mobile) Nationalist	6 August 1869	AMobM
The Mobile News	18 February 1938	AMobM
The Mobile News-Item	15 February 1932	AMobM
The Mobile Post	22 July, 12 August 1932	AMobM
The Mobile Press	From 1821 20 August 1931; 14 March 1933; 30 April 1937; 2 November 1938; 19 January 1939; 18 July, 18 October 1940; 21 February 1941; 14 August 1945; 29 June 1950; 26, 27 August 1975	AMob

AMobM |
| *The (Mobile) Public School Courier* | March, April 1936; March, December 1940; March 1941 | AMobM |
| *The Mobile Register* | From 1821 16 May 1871; 5 October 1873; 6 February 1880; 23 April 1882; 5 May 1885; 11 December 1889; 14 April 1894; 31 January 1895; 31 December 1897; 11 January, 5, 8, 14 July 1898; 1 September 1899; 28 June 1900; 6, 13, 17, 20, 23, 25, 26, 27 September, 2, 16 October, 16, 21, 26 November 1902; 16 January, 19, 22, 25, 26, 27, 28 (2) February, 3, 4, 5, | AMob |

11, 14, 15 March
1903; 1 September
1904; 23 October, 10
December 1905; 1
January, 5, 23 Feb-
ruary 1906; 1 Sep-
tember, 29
November 1908; 5
December 1909; 22
(2) May, 1 December
1910; 14 January
1912; 30 November
1913; 16 April, 6 July
1916; 11 November
1918; 31 August
1919; 27 February,
21 May 1921; 30
April 1922; 1 Sep-
tember 1924; 30 (2)
May 1926; 1 June
1924; 3 April 1927;
30 (2) January, 1
September 1928; 17
July 1932; 26
November 1933; 11
February 1934; 13
January, 7 April
1935; 3 (2) May, 21
October, 12 De-
cember 1936; 6 Oc-
tober 1937; 1 Sep-
tember, 6 December
1939; 22 January
1940; 21 (2) Feb-
ruary, 16 March
1941; 22 March 1942;
16 December 1945; 7
April 1946; 1 July, 3
August, 17 De-
cember 1950; 19
January 1952; 12 (2)
February, 4 June, 17
December 1961; 4
March 1962; 9 Au-

	gust 1974; 27 August 1975	AMobM
Mobile Register and Journal	25 February 1842; 14 March 1845	AMobM
The (Mobile) Southern Watchman	15 January 1898	AMobM
The Mobile Times	4 June 1867; 10 February, 24 March 1934; 19, 21 March 1935; 6 May 1936; 20 October 1938; 23, 24, 25, 26, 29 August 1939; 2 April 1940	AMobM
The Mobile Weekly Press	8, 15 January 1898	AMobM
The Mobile Weekly Register	7 September 1872	AMobM
(Mobile) *Witch*	31 December 1878	AMobM
(Mobile) *Young Men's Benevolent Association Herald*	1 July 1905	AMobM

Montgomery County

Alabama Journal	1952 +	AM
Montgomery Advertiser	21 July 1940 1952 +	AMobM AM
(Montgomery) *Alabama State Journal*	14 October 1868	AMobM
The Montgomery Weekly Press	15 January 1898	AMobM

Morgan County

The Decatur Daily	1970–1976 January 1973 + 1976 +	ADeW ADeD ADeW

Pike County

Brundidge newspapers	From 1893	ABrJJ
Troy newspapers	From 1866	ABrJJ

Talladega County

The (Talladega) Diocesan News	July 1918	AMobM

Tuscaloosa County

Tuscaloosa News	1975 +	AU

ALASKA

Anchorage

Anchorage News	No dates given	AkA
Anchorage Times	No dates given	AkA, AkKeHi

Cordova-McCarthy

Cordova newspapers	No dates given	AkA

Fairbanks

Fairbanks News-Miner	No dates given	AkA

Juneau

Juneau newspapers	No dates given	AkA

Kenai-Cook Inlet

Kenai newspapers	No dates given	AkA
The Peninsula Clarion (Kenai Peninsula Borough)	1970–1977	AkKeHi

Ketchikan

Ketchikan newspapers	No dates given	AkA
Ketchikan Daily News (Gateway Borough)	Pre-1970 1970–1977	AkKTHi AkKTHi

Kodiak

Kodiak newspapers	No dates given	AkA
Kodiak Fishwrapper	1975–1977	AkKoHi
Kodiak Mirror	1940–1977	AkKoHi
Kodiak Times	1975–1977	AkKoHi

Nome

Nome newspapers	No dates given	AkA

Seward

Seward newspapers	No dates given	AkA

ARIZONA

Apache County

Navajo Times	1960 +	AzFM

Coconino County

(Flagstaff) *Arizona Champion-Coconino Sun*	1883–1894	AzFU
(Flagstaff) *Arizona Daily Sun*	No dates given 1977 +	AzFM AzFU

Maricopa County

Arizona Republic	1952 +	AzPh
Phoenix Gazette	Ca. 1952–1971 1972 +	AzPh AzPh

Navajo County

Qua-Töqti	1973 +	AzFM

Pima County

Citizen	Dates not known	AzNPHi
Star	Dates not known	AzNPHi

Santa Cruz County

Herald	Dates not known	AzNPHi
International	Dates not known	AzNPHi
Oasis	Dates not known	AzNPHi
Vidette	Dates not known	AzNPHi

Yavapai County

Arizona Journal-Miner	1864–1881	AzPrSH
Prescott Courier	1977	AzPrSH

ARKANSAS

Carroll County

Carroll County Journal	No dates given	ArBerC
North Arkansas Star	No dates given	ArBerC
Star Progress	No dates given	ArBerC

CALIFORNIA

Southern California

The *Los Angeles Star Index* covers a region from San Diego north to San Luis Obispo, east to the Nevada state line, then south to the Mexican border, following the California-Nevada state line.	17 May 1851–31 December 1881	CLU-URL

Alameda County

The Berkeleyan	1874–1897	CU-BANC
Berkeley Daily Gazette	1929 +	CB
The Daily Californian	1897–1920 1921–1928 (projected) 1929 +	CU-BANC CU-BANC CU-BANC
Fremont Argus	1965 +	CFrA
Fremont News Register	1965–1972	CFrA

Calaveras County

Calaveras Weekly Chronicle	1850's–1900	CSadH
Calaveras Weekly Citizen	1850's–1900	CSadH
Mining and Scientific News	1850's–1900	CSadH

Contra Costa County

Contra Costa Times	Ca. 1935–1968 1968 +	CPlhC CPlhC
Danville Valley Pioneer	1968 +	CPlhC
Martinez Morning News Gazette	1968 +	CPlhC
Martinez News Gazette	Ca. 1935–1968	CPlhC
Oakland Tribune (Contra Costa edition)	1935–1968	CPlhC

Los Angeles County

Long Beach Independent	1959 +	CLob
Long Beach Press-Telegram	1921–1943	CLob
(Los Angeles) *Express*	1 January–30 June 1880	CLU-URL
(Los Angeles) *Herald*	2 July–27 December 1878; 4 January–27 December 1897; 1 July–31 December 1881	CLU-URL
(Los Angeles) *Semi-Weekly News*	17 November 1865–15 May 1868	CLU-URL
(Los Angeles) *Semi-Weekly Southern News*	19 July 1861–30 July 1862	CLU-URL

(Los Angeles) *Southern Californian*	20 July 1854–20 June 1855	CLU-URL
(Los Angeles) *Star*	17 May 1851–21 September 1854 (Incomplete file); 4 January 1855–1 October 1864; 16 May 1868–30 June 1878; 1 October 1878–27 May 1879	CLU-URL
**Los Angeles Times*	No dates given 1969 +	LGra CAna
(Los Angeles) *Tri-Weekly News*	1 October 1864–14 November 1865	CLU-URL

Merced County

Merced Sun Star	1 May 1977 +	CMerC

Monterey County

Carmel Pine Cone	1915 +	CCarm
Monterey Peninsula Herald	1915–1970	CCarm

Orange County

Anaheim Bulletin	1969 +	CAna
Fullerton News Tribune	1893–1928; 1961 +	CFl
(Santa Ana) *Register*	1969 +	CAna

Riverside County

(Riverside) *Daily Enterprise*	March 1973 +	CRiv
Riverside Press (Title varies)	July 1878–February 1973	CRiv

Sacramento County

Sacramento Bee	1975 +	CU-A

San Francisco

San Francisco Chronicle	No dates given	CSj
	1975 +	CU-A
San Francisco Examiner	No dates given	CSj

San Mateo County

The (San Mateo) Times	Late 1930's +	CSmatT

Santa Clara County

Daily Palo Alto Times	11 September 1958	AMobM
San Jose Mercury	No dates given	CSj
San Jose News	No dates given	CSj

Sonoma County

News Herald	1975 +	CStr
Petaluma Argus Courier	No dates given	CStr
Press Democrat	Pre-1958	CStr
	1958 +	CStr

Stanislaus County

Modesto Bee	1971 +	CMS

Yolo County

California Aggie (UC Davis)	1975 +	CU-A

Yuba County

(Marysville) *Appeal Democrat*	1960 (Centennial edition)	CMary
Marysville Daily Appeal	1854–1967	CMary
(Marysville) *Daily National Democrat*	13 August 1858	CMary
(Marysville) *Daily Northern Statesman*	26 June 1867–13 July 1867	CMary
Marysville Evening Democrat	October 1884–13 July 1886	CMary
Marysville Herald	6 August 1850–17 July 1851	CMary
The (Marysville) Northern California	17 December 1866–22 June 1867	CMary
Marysville Star and Wheatland Herald	14 August 1935–December 1936	CMary
(Marysville) *Wheatland Herald*	27 July 1934–16 August 1935	CMary
Yuba City Herald	August 1935–January 1937	CMary
Yuba City Independent Herald	August 1947 +	CMary

COLORADO

Denver County

Denver Post	1950 + (Indexed clipping file)	CoC
	1960–1977	CoStN
	1967–1977	KDcC

Lakewood Sentinel	1975 +	CoLw
Rocky Mountain News	1960–1977	CoStN

El Paso County

Colorado City Independent	21 August 1914–8 June 1917	CoC
Colorado City Iris	31 January 1891–20 August 1914	CoC
Colorado Prospector	July 1969 + (Indexed on cards)	CoC
Colorado Springs Free Press	3 February 1947– 30 December 1966	CoC
	1 January 1967–10 March 1970 (Indexed clipping file)	CoC
Colorado Springs Gazette	1 May 1878–4 February 1946	CoC
Colorado Springs Gazette Telegraph	5 February 1946 +	CoC
Colorado Springs Sun	11 March 1970 + (Indexed clipping file)	CoC
Colorado Springs Weekly Gazette	4 January 1873–26 December 1900	CoC
Evening Telegraph	1 January 1912–4 February 1946	CoC
Out West	23 March–26 December 1872	CoC

La Plata County

Durango Herald	1972 +	CoDuF

Logan County

    Sterling Journal Advocate   1960–1976   CoStN

Mesa County

    (Grand Junction) *Daily Sentinel*   No dates given   CoGjM
                                               Pre-1950   CoGj
                                               Ca. 1950 +   CoGj
                                               1972 +   CoGj
                                               1976 +   CoGj

Pueblo County

    Pueblo Chieftain   1950 + (Indexed
                                        clipping file)   CoC

    Pueblo Star-Journal   1950 + (Indexed
                                        clipping file)   CoC

CONNECTICUT

Hartford County

    (Hartford) *Connecticut Courant*   29 October 1764; 5
                                          December 1804; 30
                                          October 1805; 8 Oc-
                                          tober 1806; 6 Feb-
                                          ruary, 26 June, 7
                                          August 1811; 5 Oc-
                                          tober, 28 December
                                          1813; 13 February
                                          1816   AMobM

    (Hartford) *Connecticut Mirror*   24 December 1810; 4
                                          March, 19 August
                                          1811; 30 November
                                          1812   AMobM

The Hartford Courant	Ca. 1800 +	CtHSD
(Hartford) *The Times*	3 June 1817	AMobM
The Hartford Times	26 January, 26 October 1839	AMobM
	1850's–1976	CtHSD
Hartford Daily Courant	16 July 1870	AMobM

Litchfield County

The Winsted Herald Weekly Register	7 September 1872	AMobM

New Haven County

Colonial Connecticut newspapers	1755–1775	LNPo

New London County

Norwich Weekly Courier	12 January 1853	AMobM

DISTRICT OF COLUMBIA

National Intelligencer	1800–1850	DNGS
	20 August, 15, 27 December 1810; 2 (2), 4 May 1811; 19 September, 17 November 1812; 21 September, 12, 30 October 1813; 31 December 1814; 12 September, 22 October, 28 December 1816; 6, 27 May, 9 September, 28 October 1817; 7 July, 5	

	December 1818; 31 July, 7 August, 8 September, 16, 23 December 1819; 3 March 1821; 28 March 1822; 6 March 1823; 19 April, 30 August 1825; 21 April, 12 May 1827; 19 June, 28 October 1828; 7, 29 November 1838; 12 March, 28 September, 17 October 1839; 12 April, 26 August 1856; 3 July 1860	AMobM
National Intelligencer and Washington Advertiser	10 September 1806; 7 March 1808; 23, 25 August, 1, 8 September 1809; 16 July 1810	AMobM
**National Observer*	1964 + (Current clippings)	FNiO
The States and Union	13 November 1860	AMobM
The United States Telegraph	6, 11 October 1832	AMobM
The Universal Gazette	12 December 1805; 1 May 1806; 31 August 1809; 1 February 1811; 14 August 1812	AMobM
**Washington Post*	No dates given Ca. 1962 + 1970–1974	LGra DBRE ViAr
Washington Star	Ca. 1962 + 1973 +	DBRE ViAr

FLORIDA

Alachua County

(Gainesville) *Independent Florida Alligator* (University of Florida)	1955 +	FU

Dade County

Miami Herald	1953–1960	FM
	1961 +	FM
Miami News	1953–1960	FM
	1961 +	FM

Duval County

(Jacksonville) *Times-Union*	Date unknown +	FSaHi
	1966 +	FJU

Escambia County

Pensacola Journal	1964 + (Vertical file—in Archives)	FNiO

Hillsborough County

Tampa Tribune	1955 +	FU

Okaloosa County

Bayou Times	1970's + (In Archives)	FNiO
Okaloosa News-Journal	1964 + (In Archives)	FNiO
Playground Daily News	1964 + (Vertical file—in Archives)	FNiO

Saint Johns County

   Saint Augustine Record   1899 +   FSaHi

Walton County

   The DeFuniak Herald   1964 (In Archives)   FNiO

GEORGIA

General

   All extant Georgia newspapers   1763–1800 (Probate/
                                          estate notices)   GDanH
                                          1763–1830 (Marriages
                                          and deaths)   GDanH

Chatham County

   The Savannah Republican   8 August 1864   AMobM

Cobb County

   Cobb County area newspapers   No dates given   GMarC

DeKalb County

   Decatur-DeKalb News/Sun   1970's +   GD

   DeKalb New Era   1950's +   GD

Fulton County

   Atlanta Constitution   1920's–1974 (Clip-
                                          pings on microfiche)   GA
                                          1960's +   GD

	1971–1976 (Commercial index)	GMarC
Atlanta Journal	No dates given	ALoaLHi
	1920's–1974 (Clippings on microfiche)	GA
	1960's +	GD
	1975 + (Indexed on 3″ × 5″ cards)	GA
Atlanta Journal-Constitution	1964 + (Current clippings)	FNiO
(Atlanta) *Southern Confederacy*	29 July 1863	AMobM

Grady County

Cairo Messenger	1904 +	GCai
Grady County Progress	1912–1917	GCai
Whigham Journal	February 1909– 1 April 1910	GCai

Muscogee County

Columbus Enquirer	No dates given	ALoaLHi

Richmond County

Augusta newspapers	No dates given	GAuA
Augusta Newspaper Digest	1861; 1863–1866; 1868–1873	GAuA
Augusta Chronicle	1960 +	GAu
(Augusta) *Daily Chronicle and Sentinel*	8 November 1864	AMobM
Augusta Herald	1960 +	GAu
(Augusta) *Southern Field and Fireside*	23 April 1864	AMobM

HAWAII

Honolulu County

    Hawaii Observer   February 1973 +   HPcI

IDAHO

Eastern Idaho

    Eastern Idaho Farmer   No dates given   IdIf

Ada County

    (Boise) *Idaho Statesman*   July 1964–1972   IdB
    (Formerly *Idaho Daily Statesman*)   1973 +   IdB

    (Boise) *Intermountain Observer*   9 September 1967–20
                                         October 1973   IdPI

Bingham County

    Blackfoot News   No dates given   IdIf

    Shelley Pioneer   No dates given   IdIf

Bonneville County

    (Idaho Falls) *Post-Register*   No dates given   IdIf
                                         1949 +   IdRR

Butte County

    Arco Advertiser   No dates given   IdIf

Custer County

    Challis Messenger   No dates given   IdIf

    Mackay Miner   No dates given   IdIF

Fremont County

    Ashton Herald   No dates given   IdIf

    Fremont County Chronicle-News   No dates given   IdIf

    Saint Anthony Chronicle-Herald   1900 +   IdRR

Jefferson County

    Rigby Star   No dates given   IdIF
                        1902 +   IdRR

Madison County

    Rexburg Journal-Standard   No dates given   IdIf
                        1901 +   IdRR

ILLINOIS

Bureau County

    The (Princeton) Bureau County Patriot   18 August 1868   AMobM

Cook County

    The Chicago Times   15 February 1873   AMobM

**Chicago Tribune*	No dates given	LGra
	Ca. 1962 +	DBRE

Madison County

Alton Evening Telegraph	1833–1934	IAl

Rock Island County

(Moline and Rock Island) *Argus*	1977 +	IMolB
(Moline and Rock Island) *Daily Dispatch*	1977 +	IMolB

Sangamon County

(Springfield) *State Journal-Register* (Formerly *Illinois State Journal* and *Illinois State Register*)	1930's +	ISL

Wayne County

Prairie Pioneer	1855–1875	IFDB
Wayne County Press	1855–1875	IFDB

INDIANA

Floyd County

New Albany Tribune	Pre-1970	InNea
	1970 +	InNea

Madison County

Elwood Call-Leader	1921–1956	InElw
	1966–1971	InElw

Marion County

Indianapolis Star	1 July 1973–30 June 1976	InIS

Pulaski County

Democratic Journal	1883–Ca. 1917	InWinaCL
Pulaski County Democrat	1888–1956	InWinaCL
Pulaski County Journal	1957 +	InWinaCL
Pulaski Democrat	1858–1881	InWinaCL
Winamac Journal	1878–Ca. 1883	InWinaCL
Winamac Republican	1865–1956	InWinaCL

Vanderburgh County

Evansville newspapers	No dates given	InEM
	From 1915	InE
Evansville Courier	Ca. 1930–1977	InEM
	1 March 1972 +	InE
Evansville Courier-Press (Sunday)	Ca. 1930–1977	InEM
	1 March 1972 +	InE
Evansville Press	Ca. 1930–1977	InEM
	1 March 1972 +	InE

Warrick County

Newburgh Register	1967–1977	InEM

IOWA

General

Iowa newspapers	No dates given Ca. 1850 +	Ia-Ha IaHi Ia-NL

Southwestern Iowa

Southwestern Iowa newspapers	No dates given	NbOPC

Benton County

The Keystone Bulletin	1912–1937	IaCrCH

Black Hawk County

Cedar Falls Daily Record	1925–1977	IaCf
Cedar Falls Record	1925–1977	IaCf

Clinton County

Clinton Herald	1967 +	IaCli

Linn County

Cedear Rapids Gazette	1883–1910; 1960 +	IaCr
Mt. Vernon newspapers	January 1916– 25 December 1919 January 1922–July 1924	IaCrLC IaCrLC
Mt. Vernon and Lisbon newspapers	1922; 1923; 1932– 1936 1903–1938	IaCrLC IaCrLC

	1947–1950	IaCrLC
	January 1920– December 1921; January 1924–1926	IaCrLC

Mahaska County

   Oskaloosa Daily Herald   1889–1894; 1916;
                                      1942–1948; 1960 +   IaOskW

Polk County

   Des Moines Register

	No dates given	Ia-NL
	1900 +	IaDm
	1940 +	Ia
	1950–1975	IaAS
	1975 +	IaAS

   Des Moines Tribune

	No dates given	Ia-NL
	1900 +	IaDM
	1940 +	Ia

Poweshiek County

   Scarlet and Black (Grinnell College   1894 +   IaGG
      student newspaper)

Scott County

   (Davenport and Bettendorf) *Quad-City* 1977 +   IMolB
      Times

KANSAS

Northeastern Kansas

   Northeastern Kansas newspapers   No dates given   NbOPC

Ford County

    Dodge City Daily Globe   1920–1977   KDcC

Lyon County

    (Emporia) *Kansas News*   1857–1859   KEm

Reno County

    Hutchinson News   1967–1977   KDcC

Sedgwick County

    Wichita Eagle-Beacon   1930 +   KWi
                                    1967–1977   KDcC

Shawnee County

    Topeka Capital   1930 +   KWi
                                      1967–1977   KDcC

    Topeka Daily Capital   No dates given   K

    Topeka State Journal   No dates given   K

KENTUCKY

Daviess County

    Owensboro Messenger and Inquirer   1975–1977   KyOw

LOUISIANA

Caddo Parish

Shreveport Journal	Ca. 1970–1977	LShC
Shreveport Times (or predecessor)	1860 +	LNaN
Shreveport Times	No dates given Ca. 1970–1977 1972 +	LGra LShC̈ LSh

East Baton Rouge Parish

(Baton Rouge) *Advocate* (or predecessor)	1860's +	LNaN

Lincoln Parish

Ruston Daily Leader	No dates given	LGra

Natchitoches Parish

(Natchitoches) *Times* (or predecessor)	1860 +	LNaN

Orleans Parish

(New Orleans) *Carnival Bulletin*	25 February 1936 (Comus edition); 25 February 1936 (Rex edition)	AMobM
(New Orleans) *The Daily States*	28 April 1906	AMobM
(New Orleans) *Picayune* (or predecessor)	1850 +	LNaN

**(New Orleans) *Times-Picayune*	1972–1975	LMetJ
Ouachita Parish		
Monroe Morning World	No dates given	LGra
Rapides Parish		
(Alexandria) *Town Talk*	1920 +	LNaN
Saint Landry Parish		
Eunice News (Formerly *The New Era*)	1924–1974	LU-E

MAINE

Cumberland County		
(Portland) *Post, Eastern Argus* and many local newspapers	1880–1920	MeHi
Jenks' Portland Gazette	24 September 1804	AMobM
The Portland Gazette and Maine Advertiser	21 January 1811	AMobM
Portland Press Herald	No dates given	MeMacU
Penobscot County		
(Bangor) *Daily Commercial Advertiser*	10 September 1835	AMobM
Bangor Daily News	No dates given	MeMacU

MARYLAND

Baltimore

Baltimore Patriot	26 May 1863	AMobM
Baltimore Patriot and Commercial Gazette	19 April 1853	AMobM
Baltimore Patriot and Evening Advertiser	30 September, 10, 15 October 1814; 21 March 1815	AMobM
Federal Gazette and Baltimore Daily Advertiser	9 February 1808	AMobM
Morning Chronicle and Baltimore Advertiser	8 September 1820	AMobM
Niles' National Register	19 October, 2 November 1839	AMobM
The Sun	26 April 1841	AMobM

Charles County

Citizen News	1975 +	MdLapC
Maryland Independent	1975 +	MdLapC
Times Crescent	1975 +	MdLapC

Saint Mary's County

Enterprise	1975 +	MdLapC
Saint Mary's Guardian	1975 +	MdLapC

Washington County

| Daily Mail | 1940's + | MdHag |
| Morning Herald | 1940's + | MdHag |

Worcester County

| The Continental Correspondent | 4 April 1775–
26 March 1776 | ODaNR |

MASSACHUSETTS

Berkshire County

| The Transcript | 1844–1874 | MNoad |
| | 1930 + | MNoad |

Bristol County

New Bedford Evening Standard	1850–1932	MNBedf
New Bedford Mercury	1850–1942	MNBedf
New Bedford Times	1902–1932	MNBedf
New Bedford Standard-Times	1932–1977	MNBedf
Whalemen's Shipping List and Merchants Transcript	1843–1914	MNBedf

Essex County

(NOTE: All listings under Essex County that are followed by the symbol MHa are indexed for the towns of Haverhill, Andover, Boxford,

Methuen, Groveland, Georgetown, West Newbury, Merrimac, Newbury, Newbury Port, Amesbury, and Salisbury.)

Cape Ann Advertiser	No dates given	MGlHi
The Cynic	1836	MHa
Daily Laborer	1884–1887 (Odd numbers)	MHa
Essex Banner	1834–1888	MHa
Essex Chronicle and County Republican	1830–1832	MHa
Essex County Democrat	1859–1861	MHa
Essex Gazette	1827–1836	MHa
Essex Patriot	1817–1823	MHa
Gloucester Daily Times	No dates given	MGlHi
Guardian of Freedom	1793–1795	MHa
Haverhill Daily Bulletin	1871–1898	MHa
Haverhill Evening Gazette	1804–1947	MHa
Haverhill Federal Gazette	1798	MHa
Haverhill Gazette	1823; 1826–1827; 1837 +	MHa
Haverhill Gazette and Patriot	1824–1825	MHa
Haverhill Iris	1831–1834	MHa
Haverhill Journal	1957–1965	MHa
Haverhill Museum	1800–1804	MHa
Haverhill Social Democrat	1899–1901	MHa
Haverhill Weekly Bulletin	1872–1898	MHa

Lawrence Evening Tribune	1973–1977	NhS
Lynn newspapers	No dates given	MLy
Merrimack Intelligencer	1808–1817	MHa
Newburyport Herald	10 April 1807	AMobM
The Observer	1804–1806	MHa
(Salem) *Essex County Mercury and Weekly Salem Gazette*	17 August 1864; 26 April 1865	AMobM
(Salem) *Essex Register*	8 January, 16 February, 15, 22 October 1814; 15, 22 November 1827; 30 September, 21 October 1839	AMobM
The Salem Gazette	25 December 1810; 5, 15 October 1813; 25 April, 14 October 1814; 18 August, 12 September 1820; 21 April 1865	AMobM
The Salem Observer	18 May 1867	AMobM
The Salem Register	10 November 1803; 2 September 1847; 26 May 1851; 2 March 1865; 30 April 1866	AMobM
The Star	1836	MHa
Sunday Record	1902–1947	MHa
Tri-Weekly Publisher	1859–1878	MHa

Franklin County

(Greenfield) *Gazette and Courier*	7 January 1861	AMobM

Hampden County

    (Springfield) *Hampshire Federalist*   17, 24 January 1811   AMobM

Hampshire County

    (Northampton) *Hampshire Gazette*   25 January 1815   AMobM

Middlesex County

    The Somerville Journal   15 January 1876 +   MSo
                                1 June 1934 +   MSo

Suffolk County

    (Boston) *The Christian Citizen* (Also   24 August 1844; 21
        Worcestor)   June 1845   AMobM

    **(Boston) *Christian Science Monitor* 1974–1977   CoStN

    (Boston) *Columbian Centinel*   1784–1840   MBAt
                                    27 September 1797;
                                    30 May 1798   AMobM

    (Boston) *Columbian Centinel and*   18 February 1837   AMobM
       American Federalist

    (Boston) *Columbian Centinel and Mas-* 12 March, 16
       sachusetts Federalist   November 1803; 25
                                    January, 5 December
                                    1804; 4 December
                                    1805; 23 May 1807;
                                    16 January 1811; 29
                                    May, 2 June 1813; 8
                                    January, 5, 15 Oc-
                                    tober 1814; 22, 23,
                                    25 March, 8 April,
                                    10 October 1815   AMobM

    The (Boston) Columbian for the Coun- 21 November 1846   AMobM
       try

Boston Daily Advertiser	7, 17, 21, April 1865	AMobM
(Boston) *Daily Evening Transcript*	13 November 1833	AMobM
Boston Daily Journal	25 April 1865	AMobM
(Boston) *Gazette*	1719–1798	MBAt
The Boston Gazette and Country Journal	12 March 1770	AMobM
(Boston) *Gleason's Pictorial*	23 August, 13 September 1851	AMobM
(Boston) *Independent Chronicle*	24 January 1811; 16 June 1814	AMobM
(Boston) *Independent Chronicle and Boston Patriot*	9 September, 18 November 1835; 22 April, 3 May 1837	AMobM
Boston Investigator	29 September 1854	AMobM
The (Boston) Liberator	29 August, 10 October 1856	AMobM
(Boston) *Massachusetts Centinel*	1784–1840	MBAt
(Boston) *New England Palladium*	4 April 1806; 19 June 1807; 28 August 1810; 28 January 1812	AMobM
Boston Patriot	16 January, 8 May, 25 December 1811; 2 June 1813; 13 October 1814; 25 March 1815	AMobM
Boston Post	16, 17, 20, 22 May 1867	AMobM
Boston Semi-Weekly Advertiser	9 July, 10, 13, 17 August, 17 Sep-	

	tember 1864; 8 April 1865	AMobM
The (Boston) Weekly Messenger	24, 31 March, 7 April 1815	AMobM
Boston Weekly Transcript	17 August 1864	AMobM

Worcester County

The Christian Citizen (Worcester and Boston)	24 August 1844; 21 June 1845	AMobM
(Worcester) *National Aegis*	23 November 1803	AMobM

MICHIGAN

Bay County

Bay City newspapers	Coverage varies	Mi
Bay City Times	1935–1954 1955 +	MiBay MiBay

Berrien County

Benton Harbor Herald-Palladium	No dates given	MiDecCL

Branch County

Coldwater newspapers	Coverage varies	Mi

Genesee County

Flint newspapers	Coverage varies	Mi
Flint Journal	1935 +	MiFliJ

Hillsdale County

   Hillsdale Daily News   February 1847–
                                 December 1889   MiJoBM

   Hillsdale Whig Standard   February 1847–
                                 December 1889   MiJoBM

Ingham County

   Lansing Journal   1888–1910   MiL

   Lansing Republican   1855–1910   MiL

   Lansing State Journal   1911 +   MiL
                                 1955 +   Mi

Kalamazoo County

   Kalamazoo newspapers   Coverage varies   Mi

   Kalamazoo Gazette   No dates given   MiDecCL

Kalkaska County

   Kalkaskian and Leader   1975   MiGrSE

Macomb County

   (Mount Clemens) *Macomb Daily*   1972–1977   MiScs

Saint Clair County

   Port Huron Times Herald   1930's +   MiPh

Saint Joseph County

   Three Rivers newspapers   Coverage varies   Mi

Van Buren County

   Decatur Republican   No dates given   MiDecCL

Wayne County

Detroit newspapers	Coverage varies	Mi
Detroit Free Press	No dates given 1955 +	MiFd Mi
Detroit News	No dates given 1955 +	NiFd Mi
(Ferndale) *Daily Tribune*	No dates given	MiFd
Ferndale Gazette-Times	No dates given	MiFd
Wyandotte News-Herald (Absorbed *Wyandotte Herald*)	8 October 1880– December 1881; 2 July 1886–1892; 1895–October 1896; 1897 +	MiWy
Wyandotte Tribune (Absorbed by the *Wyandotte News-Herald*)	1939–1961	MiWy

---

MISSISSIPPI

Bolivar County

(Camp Shelby) *The Reveille*	22 April 1942	AMobM

Marshall County

Marshall Messenger	No dates given	MsHos
South Reporter	Late 1960's +	MsHos

Warren County

The Vicksburg Daily Citizen (Original—on reverse side of wallpaper)	2 July 1863	OMenLHi

(Facsimile)	2 July 1863	AMobM
Vicksburg Evening Post	1960's +	MsV

Washington County

Deer Creek Pilot	1970 +	MsGW
(Greenville) *Delta Democrat Times*	1960's +	MsGW
Leland Progress	1970 +	MsGW

MISSOURI

General

All available Missouri newspapers	Pre-1850 (Scattered dates)	MoSLS
(Saint Louis) *Missouri Gazette*	1820–1825	MoSLS
(Saint Louis) *Missouri Republican*	1820–1825	MoSLS

Northwestern Missouri

Northwestern Missouri newspapers	No dates given	NbOPC

Southwestern Missouri

Springfield Daily News	1927 +	MoSp
Springfield Leader-Press	1886 +	MoSp

Andrew County

Savannah Reporter	1852–1920 (Obituaries)	MoSavHi
	1876–1899 (Births)	MoSavHi

Caldwell County

   Hamiltonian   From 1820's   MoLaSS

Cape Girardeau County

   Southeast Missourian   1968 +   MoCg

Clay County

   The (Excelsior Springs) Daily Standard No dates given   MoExGS

Cole County

   Jefferson City Post Tribune   1966 +   MoJcT

Greene County

   Springfield newspaper   2 November 1969 + MoSpLW

   Springfield Daily News   1927 +   MoSp

   Springfield Leader-Press   1886 +   MoSp

Jackson County

   Kansas City Star and Times   1967–1977   KDcC

Missouri County

   Hamiltonian   Frm 1820's   MoLaSS

Ray County

   Hamiltonian   From 1820's   MoLaSS

St. Louis

   Missouri Gazette   1808–1849   MoSLS

Missouri Republican	1808–1849	MoSLS
Saint Louis Globe-Democrat	9, 10, 13 July 1937	AMobM

Saline County

Saline County newspapers	1870's–Ca. 1925	MoGSS

MONTANA

General

Assorted Montana newspapers	Mid-1870's +	MtHi

Cascade County

Great Falls Tribune	July 1972 +	MtU

Missoula County

The Missoulian	July 1972 +	MtU

Yellowstone County

Billings Gazette	No dates given	MtG
	1930–1949	MtBilE
	1976	MtBilE

NEBRASKA

General

All Nebraska newspapers	No dates given	NbOPC

Adams County

NOTE: Although individual dates are not known for the following Hastings newspapers, the overall scope of the index is 1872–1938.

Hastings Daily Gazette-Journal	Dates unknown	NbH
Hastings Daily Republican	Dates unknown	NbH
Hastings Daily Spotlight	Dates unknown	NbH
Hastings Daily Tribune	Dates unknown	NbH
Hastings Journal	Dates unknown	NbH
Hastings Weekly Democrat	Dates unknown	NbH
Hastings Weekly Gazette-Journal	Dates unknown	NbH
Hastings Weekly Tribune	Dates unknown	NbH

Douglas County

Omaha Sun	Pre-1930's +	NbO
Omaha World Herald	Pre-1930's + 1976 +	NbO NbKS

Gage County

Beatrice Daily Sun	1968–1977	NbB

Lancaster County

Lincoln Evening Journal	1976 +	NbKS

NEW HAMPSHIRE

Carroll County

Sandwich Reporter	1887–1903	NhCsM

Grafton County

The (Hanover) American	19 June 1816	AMobM
(Hanover) *Dartmouth Gazette*	8 December 1819	AMobM

Hillsborough County

Nashua Telegraph	Retrospective	NhNa
	July 1971 +	NhNa

Merrimack County

Concord Evening Monitor (and predecessors)	1790–1920	NhC
Concord Gazette	18 October 1814; 11 April 1815	AMobM
(Concord) *New Hampshire Patriot*	16 July, 13 August 1811; 22 June 1813; 25 October 1814	AMobM
(Concord) *New Hampshire Statesman*	4 December 1858	AMobM
(Concord) *New Hampshire Statesman and State Journal*	27 September 1834	AMobM

Rockingham County

Essex County, MA newspapers have been indexed for news concerning	1793 +	MHa

the towns of Atkinson, Plaistow, Danville, Kensington, and Kingston.

(Exeter) *Constitutionalist*	7 January 1811; 20 April 1815	AMobM
Exeter Watchman	10 March 1818	AMobM
Portsmouth Herald	1977 +	NhPo
(Portsmouth) *New Hampshire Gazette*	15 November 1842	AMobM
The (Portsmouth) War Journal	11 June 1813	AMobM
Salem Observer	1973–1977	NhS

Strafford County

Rochester Courier	1976	NhR

NEW JERSEY

Bergen County

Ridgewood News	1974–1976	NjRw
Sunday News	1974–1976	NjRw

Burlington County

Mount Holly Herald	1837–1842; January–June 1860; Will continue	NjMhB
New Jersey Gazette	1777–1786 (In process)	NjMhB

Camden County

Suburban	1969–1977	NjCo
Weekly Retrospect	1969–1977	NjCo

Essex County

Montclair Times	1961 +	NjMon
West Essex Tribune	1959 +	NjLi

Mercer County

(Trenton) *New Jersey Gazette*	14 June 1780	AMobM
(Trenton) *The True American*	25 May 1822	AMobM

Middlesex County

(New Brunswick) *Home News*	1900 +	NjNb
(New Brunswick) *Sunday Times*	1900–1925	NjNb

Morris County

(Morristown) *Daily Record*	1977 +	NjWhiM
The *(Morristown) Palladium of Liberty* (A free press).	9 July 1812	AMobM

NEW MEXICO

Bernalillo County

Albuquerque Journal	1963–1977	Nm

Eddy County

Carlsbad Current-Argus	1940–1968	NmC

Otero County

Alamogordo Daily News	No dates given	NmAl

Santa Fe County

New Mexican	1963–1977	Nm

NEW YORK

Albany County

Albany Argus	Late 1800's, early 1900's	NAlI
Albany Evening Journal	Late 1800's, early 1900's	NAlI
Knickerbocker News	1930 +	NAlI
The Log Cabin (New York and Albany)	26 September 1840	AMobM
Times-Union	1930 +	NalI

Broome County

Binghamton newspapers	No dates given	NBi

Cayuga County

All newspapers in Cayuga County	1816 +	NAuHi

Erie County

Buffalo Evening News	No dates given	NBu
Courier Express	No dates given	NBu

Herkimer County

Herkimer County newspapers	1825–1900	NHerkCHi

Moore County

13 Rochester newspapers	1818–1850	NR
5 Rochester newspapers	1851–1897	NR
Democrat and Chronicle	1930 +	NRGR
Times-Union	1930 +	NRGR

Nassau County

Glen Cove Gazette	1857–1896 (Books 1–21)	NEh
Nassau Daily Review	1921–1937	NEmNHi
Nassau Daily Star	1927–1937	NEmNHi
Newsday	1957 +	NEmNHi

New York County

New York newspapers	1900–1970	PPFr
The New York American	14 May 1828; 8 September 1835	AMobM
The (New York) Columbian for the Country	20 April 1811; 21 November 1812	AMobM

The New York Daily Times	30 September, 6 October 1856; 1, 2 February 1858; 6 July, 11, 15, 16, 29, 30 August, 1, 2, 6 September 1864; 6, 7 (2) April 1865; 25 September 1866; 13 November, 27 December 1867; 28 March 1868; 7 August 1869; 14, 18 April 1873; 11 November 1880	AMobM
The New York Daily Tribune	7 December 1848; 21 April 1851; 26 August 1852; 22 September 1853; 30 August 1856; 22 September, 23 November 1860; 3, 21 June 1861; 17, 18 March, 17 June 1862; 26 May 1863; 19 February, 30 March, 18 April, 7 July, 5, 9, 10, 11, 12, 15, 16, 17, 20, 22, 23, 27 August, 17 September, 3 October 1864; 20 January, 10, 17 February, 29 March, 19 September, 3 October 1865; 11 April 1866; 28, 31 May, 11 June 1867; 4 February, 22 April, 14 November 1868; 7 August 1869; 16 April 1873	AMobM
(New York) *Dollar Weekly Herald*	12 November 1849	AMobM

**The New York Evening Post*	26 November 1805; 19 November 1812; 18 August 1826; 3 October, 17 December 1863; 9, 11, 12, 16 August, 1, 15 September, 10, 14, 22 October, 11 November 1864; 29 March 1865	AMobM
(New York) *Frank Leslie's Illustrated Newspaper* (For the most part, items listed are single pages of lithographics about battle and post-Civil War pictures of Mobile)	16 March, 13 April, 22 June 1861; 25 January, 17 May, 7 June, 13 September 1862; 14 March, 23 (2) May, 1, 15 August 1863; 2 January, 2 April, 15, 29 October, 5 November, 17 December 1864; 17 July, 4 November 1865; 18 October 1879; 13 March, 17 April 1886	AMobM
(New York) *Gazette of the United States* (Reproduction)	29 April–2 May 1789	AMobM
(New York) *Harper's Pictorial History of the Civil War*	Volume I and II	AMobM
(New York) *Harper's Weekly* (Most items are single pages of illustrations)	12 June 1858; 9 February, 30 March, 13, 27 April, 18, 25 May, 15, 22 June, 27 July, 17 August, 28 September, 19, 26 October, 21 December 1861; 1, 8 February, 29 March, 5 April, 17, 31 May, 16 August, 25 October, 1,	

15 November 1862;
3, 17 January, 28
February, 21 (2)
March, 25 April, 2
May, 29 August, 21
November, 5 De-
cember 1863; 30
January, 13, 20 Feb-
ruary, 12, 19, 26
March, 9, 16 April,
14 May, 16, 23 July,
6, 20 August, 3, 10,
17, 24 September, 8,
22, 29 October, 5, 26
November, 10, 17
December 1864; 13,
25 February, 25
March, 15, 29 April,
6, 27 May, 24 June,
15 July, 26 August, 2
October 1865; 8 Sep-
tember 1866; 2 Feb-
ruary, 31 May 1884;
23 May 1885; 16 July
1887; 25 February
1888   AMobM

The New York Herald

15 Septembet 1804;
27 November, 18
December 1805; 2,
30 January, 10 Au-
gust, 25 September
1811; 21 November
1812; 19 October
1814; 25 March 1815;
6 November 1835; 1
May 1837; 6 April, 3,
4 May 1842; 19
March, 2 July, 19
September 1854; 21
January, 23, 25 Au-
gust 1856; 3 Feb-
ruary, 14 December
1858; 14 January
1861; 14 May 1862;

	13 January, 26 February, 14 August, 15 September 1863; 9, 24, 27 February, 11 March, 10, 17, 29 August, 2, 6 September 1864; 15 April, 10 June, 11 August 1865; 29 December 1873; 31 October 1874; 22 January 1899	AMobM
The New York Home Journal	30 May 1857	AMobM
The New York Illustrated News	1 November 1862	AMobM
The New York Independent	18 August 1864; 25 March 1886	AMobM
The New York Journal and Advertiser	12 December 1897	AMobM
The New York Journal of Commerce	8 August 1835 Ca. 1962 +	AMobM DBRE
The (New York) Log Cabin (Also Albany)	26 September 1840	AMobM
The New York Mercury	30 March 1831	AMobM
(New York) *National Anti-Slavery Standard*	30 January, 20 February 1858; 10 October 1863; 15 July 1865; 25 August 1866; 1, 22 June, 7 December 1867; 29 February 1868	AMobM
New York Post-Boy	1743–1773	DNGS
The New York Spectator	23 May 1806	AMobM
(New York) *The Spirit of the Times*	9 June 1860	AMobM
The New York Statesman	12 November 1827	AMobM

The (New York) Sun	3 September 1833; 23 February 1864; 2 September 1933	AMobM
**New York Times*	Current	NjLi
	No dates given	LGra
	1851–1975	LMetJ
	1915 +	CoC
	1952 +	AAnn
	Ca. 1962 +	DBRE
	1964+	
	(Current clippings)	FNiO
	1971–1975	
	(Commercial index)	GMarC
	1974 +	TxJaL
**(New York) *Wall Street Journal*	Ca. 1962 +	DBRE
	1964 +	AAnn
	1964 +	
	(Current clippings)	FNiO
(New York) *The War*	21 November 1812; 1 June, 19 October 1813; 26 April 1814	AMobM
The New York Weekly Tribune	22 October 1842; 18 February 1843; 13 February 1847	AMobM
The (New York) World	6 August, 27 December 1864; 31 March, 5, 17 June 1865; 22 November 1882; 22 August 1883	AMobM

Niagara County

Iris of Niagara	Scattered 19th century issues	NNia
Lewiston Sentinel	No dates given	NNia
Niagara County News	No dates given	NNia

Niagara Falls Gazette	1854 +	NNia
Niagara Falls Journal	Scattered 19th century issues	NNia
Suspension Bridge Journal	Scattered 19th century issues	NNia
Wilson Star	No dates given	NNia
Youngstown News	No dates given	NNia

Oneida County

Rome Sentinel	1830–1977	NRomHi

Onondaga County

Syracuse Herald Journal	1962 +	NSyCM
Syracuse Post Standard	1962 +	NSyCM

Ontario County

Geneva newspapers	1806–1900	NGHi

Rensselaer County

American Spy	1791–1797	NT
Federal Herald	1788–1790	NT
Lansingburgh Advertiser	1787–1788	NT
Lansingburgh Chronicle	No dates given	NT
Lansingburgh Courier	1865–1894	NT
Lansingburgh Daily Gazette	1860	NT

Lansingburgh Democrat	1844–1861	NT
Lansingburgh Gazette	1798–1883	NT
Lansingburgh Times	1887–1895	NT
Northern Centinel	1787–1788	NT
Troy Budget	1797–1860	NT
Troy Gazette	1802–1810	NT
Troy Sentinel	1823–1832	NT
Troy Times	1851–1860	NT
Troy Whig	1834–1860	NT

Richmond County

Staten Island Advance	1885 +	NNSIHi

Saint Lawrence County

Ogdensburg Journal	Ca. 1857–1930	NOg

Suffolk County

East Hampton Star	1885–1970	NEh
Long Islander	1839–1845	NHuHi
	1839–1864; 1865–1881	
	(Marriages and deaths)	NHuHi
Newsday	1970's	NSm
Sag Harbor Corrector	1822–1888	NEh
Smithtown Messenger	1970's	NSm

Smithtown News	1970's	NSm

Ulster County

(Kingston) *Ulster County Gazette* (Fac-simile)	4 January 1800	AMobM

NORTH CAROLINA

General

All extant North Carolina newspapers	1770–1783 (Marriages, deaths, individual notices)	GDanH
Raleigh Register and North Carolina State Gazette	1799–1893	NcW

Southeastern North Carolina

All newspapers listed under Hanover County can be considered as indexed for southeastern North Carolina.

Buncombe County

Asheville Messenger	Ca. 1849–1852	NcRGS
Asheville News	1851–1869	NcRGS
Asheville Pioneer	1865–1870	NcRGS
Asheville Spectator	1853–1858	NcRGS
Asheville Times	1965 +	NcMHi
Highland Messenger	1840–Ca. 1849	NcRGS
Messenger	1842–1843	NcRGS

North Carolina Citizen	February 1870–June 1870	NcRGS

Catawba County

Hickory Daily Record	1941–1977	NcHy

Durham County

Carolina Times	1920's +	NcDur
Durham Morning Herald	1920's +	NcDur
Durham Sun	1920's +	NcDur

New Hanover County

Cape Fear Recorder	1829–1832	NcW
Commercial	No date	NcW
Peoples Press	1832–1833	NcW
Peoples Press and Wilmington Advertiser	1835–1836	NcW
Wilmington Advertiser	1837–1839; 1841–1842	NcW
Wilmington Chronicle	1840–1842	NcW
Wilmington Gazette	1803–1811	NcW

NORTH DAKOTA

Barnes County

(Valley City) *Times Record*	No dates given	NdVcT

Burleigh County

Bismarck Tribune	No dates given	NdVcT
	1952 +	NdMayS

Cass County

Fargo Forum	No dates given	NdVcT
	1952 +	NdMayS

Grand Forks County

Grand Forks Herald	1952 +	NdMayS

Traill County

Traill County Tribune	1952 +	NdMayS

OHIO

Allen County

Lima Citizen	1957–1962	OLimaM
Lima News	1909 +	OLimaM

Ashtabula County

Ashtabula Telegraph and Lake County Free Press	1851, 1852	OMenLHi
Ashtabula Weekly Telegraph and Lake County Advertiser	1851, 1852	OMenLHi
Conneaut Reporter	18 January 1849	OMenLHi

Cuyahoga County

Cleveland newspapers	No dates given	OMenLHi
Cleveland Public Library Index to Cleveland Newspapers	January 1976 +	OClPD
**Annals of Cleveland (Indexes at times—*Cleveland Register, Cleveland Herald, Cleveland Whig, Cleveland Herald and Gazette, Cleveland Daily True Democrat, Forest City Democrat, Cleveland Leader*)	1818–1875 (On film)	OClPD

**Cleveland Plain Dealer*	No dates given	OFph
	1850–1950 (Necrology file)	OClPD
	1908–1940 (Picture and card index)	OClPD
	1908 + (Clippings)	OClPD
	1931; 1933–1938 (Partial index)	OClPD
	April–November 1971 (Index by Case Western Reserve University)	OClPD

Darke County

Stillwater Valley Advertiser	1976 (Bicentennial Review Edition)	ODaNR

Delaware County

Delaware Gazette	1976 +	ODCL

Erie County

Sandusky newspaper	1822–1850	ONorHT

Franklin County

(Columbus) *Citizen-Journal*	No dates given	OCoG
(Columbus) *Dispatch*	No dates given	OCoG
Tri-Village News	No dates given	OCoG
Upper Arlington News	No dates given	OCoG

Geauga County

(Chardon) *Geauga Democrat*	1868–1869	OMenLHi
Geauga Gazette	No dates given	OMenLHi
Geauga Republican	1904	OMenLHi

Hamilton County

Cincinnati Daily Commercial	29 April, 17 October 1862; 15 September 1863; 14 December 1864; 21, 29 March, 11, 12, 13, 14, 18 April, 10, 19, 23, 31 May, 16 October, 12 December 1865	AMobM
Cincinnati Daily Gazette	23 May 1965	AMobM
**Cincinnati Enquirer*	No dates given 7 November 1897	OCHP AMobM
(Cincinnati) *Liberty Hall*	23 November 1813; 11 January 1814	AMobM
Cincinnati Post	No dates given	OCHP
Cincinnati Times-Star	No dates given	OCHP

Huron County

Three Norwalk newspapers	1827–1850	ONorHT

Lake County

Ashtabula Telegraph and Lake County Free Press	1851, 1852	OMenLHi
Ashtabula Weekly Telegraph and Lake County Advertiser	1851, 1852	OMenLHi
Chambers Journal	5 October 1891 (Volume I, #1)	OMenLHi
Daily Republican	1903, 1906	OMenLHi
Daily Telegraph	5 September 1878	OMenLHi
Evening Advertiser	14 November 1893 (Volume I, #12)	OMenLHi
Evening Telegraph	14 November 1893 (Volume II, #22)	OMenLHi
Fairport Beacon (Now defunct)	No dates given	OFph OMenLHi
Grand River Record	26 February 1853	OMenLHi
Lake County Advertiser	1895, 1898	OMenLHi
Lake County Herald	1920	OMenLHi
Lake County Weekly Herald	1909, 1910	OMenLHi
Madison Index	No dates given	OMenLHi
Madison Monitor	No dates given	OMenLHi
Mentor Monitor	No dates given	OMenLHi
Northern Ohio Journal	1880	OMenLHi

(Painesville) *Advertiser*	1868, 1871, 1875, 1881, 1882 (Issues in these years)	OMenLHi
(Painesville) *Astonisher*	1893 (Volume XI, #19)	OMenLHi
(Painesville) *Daily Issue*	23, 26, 29, 30 October, 1 November 1909 (#1)	OMenLHi
Painesville Democrat	1884, 1886, 1892	OMenLHi
Painesville Journal	1872, 1886, 1892	OMenLHi
Painesville Telegraph (Under various names)	No dates given	OFph OMenLHi
	1822 +	OPaM
Willoughby Gazette	1870	OMenLHi
Willoughby Independent	1881, 1885, 1888, 1894, 1895, 1902	OMenLHi
(Willoughby) *New Herald*	No dates given	OMenLHi

Miami County

Stillwater Valley Advertiser	1976 (Bicentennial Review Edition)	ODaNR

Montgomery County

Dayton Daily News	Ca. 1937 +	ODa
Dayton Journal Herald	Ca. 1937 +	ODa

Preble County

Eaton Democrat	Pre-1850	OWesaJG
	1850–1907	OWesaJG

Eaton Register	Pre-1850	OWesaJG
	1850–1907	OWesaJG

Ross County

(Chillicothe) *The Weekly Recorder*	26 March 1819	AMobM

Scioto County

Portsmouth Evening Tribune	3 November 1853–10 November 1860	OPosm
Portsmouth Times	September 1858–1868	OPosm
Portsmouth Union and Times	1860–1865	OPosm
Portsmouth Western Times	6 July 1826–13 December 1827	OPosm

Warren County

Franklin Gazette	No dates given (33 rolls)	OLeWHi
Warren County Reporter	No dates given (12 rolls)	OLeWHi
Waynesville Gazette	No dates given (25 rolls)	OLeWHi
Western Star	1807–1976	OLeWHi

OKLAHOMA

Carter County

Daily Ardmoreite	1940's +	OkAr
	1968–1977	OkAr

Cherokee County

Cherokee County Chronicle	1972 +	OkTahN
Pictorial Press	1963 +	OkTahN
Star Citizen	1936 +	OkTahN
The Tahlequah Citizen	1936 +	OkTahN
Times	No dates given	OkTahN

Muskogee County

Muskogee Daily Phoenix	1970 +	OkTahN

Oklahoma County

Daily Oklahoman	1930 +	OkOk
	1940's +	OkAr
	1968 +	OkAr
Oklahoma City Times	1930 +	OkOk
Oklahoma Journal	1960 +	OkOk
The Oklahoman	1967–1977	KDcC

Okmulgee County

Okmulgee Daily Times	1968 +	OkOkm

OREGON

Clatsup County

Astoria newspapers	1962 +	OrAst

Daily Astorian	Current (Indexing started)	OrAst

Lane County

(Eugene) *Register-Guard*	No dates given	OrENC
Springfield Valley News	No dates given	OrENC

PENNSYLVANIA

Adams County

(Gettysburg) *Compiler*	1818–1885	PGCoHi
(Gettysburg) *Sentinel*	1800–1885	PGCoHi

Allegheny County

(Homestead) *Amerikansky Russky Viestnik*	1894–1914	MnU-IA
(Pittsburgh) *Daily Union*	21 April 1853	AMobM

Berks County

Reading Eagle	1900–June 1936	PR

Chester County

Chester County newspapers	1800's and 1900's	PWcHi

Cumberland County

(Carlisle) *American Volunteer*	1814–1878	PCarlH
(Carlisle) *Evening Sentinel*	1874–1885	PCarlH

Carlisle Gazette	1785–1817	PCarlH
Carlisle Herald	1802–1815; 1829–1850	PCarlH
(Carlisle) *Pennsylvania Statesman*	1842–1845	PCarlH
Carlisle Republican	1823–1838	PCarlH

Dauphin County

Harrisburg Argus	27 May 1846	AMobM

Delaware County

Chester Times	No dates given	PCDHi
Delaware County Republican	1833–1888	PCDHi
Delaware County Times	No dates given	PCDHi

Lancaster County

Intelligencer Journal	1900–1960	PLMHi
	Ca. 1960 +	PLMHi
New Era	Ca. 1970 +	PLMHi
Sunday News	Ca. 1972 +	PLMHi

Luzerne County

(Wilkes-Barre) *Record of the Times*	1 December 1858; 8 May 1867; 4 May 1877	AMobM

Montgomery County

(Sumneytown) *Bauern Freund*	1830–1861	PPeSchw

Philadelphia County

Philadelphia newspapers	1900–1970	PPFr
Almanac	Ca. 1898–1955	PU
	1955–1958	PU
	1968 +	PU
Columns	Ca. 1898–1855	PU
	1955–1958	PU
	1968 +	PU
Daily Pennsylvanian	Ca. 1898–1955	PU
	1955–1958	PU
	1968 +	PU
Germantown Telegraph	March 1830–August 1833	PPGHi
Library Chronicle	Ca. 1898–1955	PU
	1955–1958	PU
	1968 +	PU
Penn Press (Title varies)	Ca. 1898–1955	PU
	1955–1958	PU
	1968 +	PU
Pennsylvania Chronicle	1767–1774	DNGS
Pennsylvania Gazette (and Predecessors)	Ca. 1898–1955	PU
	1955–1958	PU
	1968 +	PU
Pennsylvania Triangle	Ca. 1898–1955	PU
	1955–1958	PU
	1968 +	PU
(Philadelphia) *Atkinson's Saturday Evening Post*	2 November 1833; 26 October 1839	AMobM
(Philadelphia) *The Democratic Press*	8 June 1813	AMobM
(Philadelphia) *Dunlap's Pennsylvania Packet or The General Advertiser* (Facsimile)	8 July 1776	AMobM

(Philadelphia) *The Family Messenger and National Gleaner*	6 June 1849	AMobM
(Philadelphia) *Franklin Gazette*	10 December 1818	AMobM
(Philadelphia) *The General Advertiser, Aurora for the Country*	3, 15 December 1805; 21 (2) February 1806; 22, 24 May 1813; 5 January, 28 March, 13 June, 11, 17 October 1814	AMobM
The Philadelphia Inquirer	12 March, 6 July, 3, 9, 11, 15, 16, 20, 29, 30 August, 2 September 1864; 14 February, 31 March, 27 November 1865; 28 May 1866; 15, 16 May 1867; 23 July 1869	AMobM
(Philadelphia) *National Gazette and Literary Register*	27 July 1822; 24 June 1823; 30 December 1830	AMobM
(Philadelphia) *The Pennsylvanian for the Country*	22, 24, 29 October 1839	AMobM
(Philadelphia) *Poulson's American Daily Advertiser*	27 May 1813	AMobM
The Philadelphia Press	22 June 1861	AMobM
(Philadelphia) *Public Ledger* (Reproduction)	25 March 1836	AMobM
The Philadelphia Saturday Courier	26 October 1839	AMobM
(Philadelphia) *The Union, United States Gazette and True American for the Country*	2 September 1813; 12 August 1818; 16 October 1821	AMobM
(Philadelphia) *The United States Gazette*	12 September 1826; 13 November 1827	AMobM

(Philadelphia) *The Weekly North American*	19 October, 2 November 1839	AMobM

Westmoreland County

Ligonier Echo	1896–1977	PLig

York County

Evening Herald	1894–1904	PHan
Hanover Citizen	1861–1878	PHan
Hanover Evening Sun	1915 +	PHan
Hanover Herald	1835–1839; 1872–1916	PHan
Hanover Spectator	1844–1893	PHan
Record Herald	1904–1930	PHan

RHODE ISLAND

Newport County

Newport Daily News	1976 +	RN

Providence County

Manufacturers' and Farmers' Journal and Providence and Pawtucket Advertiser	11 September 1820; 22 November 1827; 20 February 1845	AMobM
Providence Daily Journal	10, 16, 20, 23, 25 August, 1, 10, 21	

	September 1864; 3, 7, 13, 27 April 1865	AMobM
Providence Gazette	11 April 1821	AMobM
Providence Patriot, Columbian Phoenix	22 October 1814	AMobM

SOUTH CAROLINA

General

| All extant South Carolina newspapers | 1733–1783 (Marriages, deaths, individual notices) | GDanH |

Charleston County

| *News and Courier* | No dates given | ScCMu |

York County

| *Evening Herald* | Pre-1940 | ScRhY |
| | 1940 + | ScRhY |

SOUTH DAKOTA

Brookings County

| Brookings newspaper | No dates given | SdBroU |
| *Brookings Register* | 20 June 1890– January 1977 | SdBro |

Minnehaha County

   Sioux Falls Argus Leader   No dates given   SdBroU

Tripp County

   Winner Advocate   1949–1977   SdWinT

TENNESSEE

Knox County

Knoxville Journal	1890's–Ca. 1960	TKL
	Ca. 1960 +	TKL
Knoxville News-Sentinel	1890's–Ca. 1960	TKL
	Ca. 1960 +	TKL

Shelby County

Commercial Appeal	Late 1960's +	MsHos
The Memphis Daily Appear	11 May 1862	AMobM

TEXAS

General

   Various Texas newspapers   No dates given
                                  (Some very early)   TxSaDR

Panhandle Area

Amarillo Daily News	1931–1937; 1960– 1977	TxAM
Amarillo Globe Times	1931–1937; 1960– 1977	TxAM
Amarillo News Globe	14 August 1938 (Special edition)	TxAM
Amarillo Sunday News Globe	1895–1930 (All available issues) 1931–1937; 1960– 1977	TxAM TxAM

Bexar County

San Antonio Express	Late 1800's +	TxSaDR
San Antonio Light	Late 1800's +	TxSaDR

Dallas County

Dallas Morning News	1900's (Various dates)	TxSaDR

Galveston County

(Galveston) *Daily News*	1865 +	TxGR
(Galveston) *Flake's Bulletin*	1865–1872	TxGR
(Galveston) *Tribune*	1885–1964	TxGR
(Galveston) *Tri-Weekly News*	1855–1873	TxGR

Harris County

Houston Post	1976 +	TxJaL

Lubbock County

The West Texas Times	November 1976 +	
	(Friday edition)	TxLMC
	April 1977 +	
	(Wednesday edition)	TxLMC

McLennan County

Waco Herald Tribune	1970–1975	TxW

Nacogdoches County

The Pioneer of Deep East Texas (for- merly *The Deep East Texas Pioneer Regional Weekly*)	August 1976 +	TxLMC

Potter County

Amarillo Daily News	1931–1937; 1960– 1977	TxAm
Amarillo Globe Times	1931–1937; 1960– 1977	TxAm
Amarillo News Globe	14 August 1938 (Special edition)	TxAm
Amarillo Sunday News Globe	1895–1930 (All available issues)	TxAm
	1931–1937; 1960– 1977	TxAm

Taylor County

Abilene Daily Reporter	1904–1920	TxAb
Abilene Reporter	1888–1900	TxAb
Abilene Reporter News	1975 +	TxAb

UTAH

Salt Lake County

Deseret News	Ca. 1950 + (Clip-pings)	USl
	1976–1977	UP
Salt Lake Tribune	1943 + (Index)	USl
	Ca. 1950 +	USl
	1976–1977	UP

Utah County

The Daily Herald	1976–1977	UP

VERMONT

General

Miscellaneous Vermont newspapers	No dates given	VtA

Bennington County

Bennington Banner	No dates given	VtA

Rutland County

Rutland Herald	No dates given	VtA

Windham County

Bellows Falls Gazette	7 November 1840	AMobM

Windsor County

Eagle Times	Pre-1930	VtSf
(or predecessors)	1930 +	VtSf

VIRGINIA

General

Richmond News Leader	1941 +	Vi
Richmond Times-Dispatch	1941 +	Vi

Alexandria

Alexandria Gazette	1950's +	ViAl

Appomattox County

Times-Virginian	No dates given	ViApCL

Arlington County

Arlington Journal	1973 +	ViAr
Arlington News	1973 +	ViAr
Northern Virginia Sun	1970 +	ViAr

Henrico County

Richmond Times-Dispatch	1973 +	ViAr

Norfolk

| *Norfolk Ledger Star* | 1963 + | ViPo |
| *Norfolk Virginian Pilot* | 1963 + | ViPo |

Richmond

Religious Herald (State paper of Virginia Baptists)	1828–1873	ViRVB
(Richmond) *Daily Dispatch*	12 August 1864	AMobM
Richmond Enquirer	1804–1859 (Marriages and obituaries)	Vi
	10 September 1813; 30 May, 22 July, 9 September 1817; 3 November 1818; 19 August 1823; 21 August 1827	AMobM
The Richmond Examiner	12, 27 August 1864	AMobM
Richmond News Leader	1941 +	Vi
Richmond Times-Dispatch	1941 +	Vi
Richmond Whig	1804–1859 (Marriages)	Vi
	1824–1859 (Obituaries)	Vi
Visitor	1809–1810 (Marriages and obituaries)	Vi

WASHINGTON

Spokane County

Spokane Daily Chronicle	Ca. 1890–1977	WaSpHiE
Spokane Spokesman Review	Ca. 1890–1977	WaSpHiE

WEST VIRGINIA

Kanawha County

Charleston Daily Mail	1950 +	WvC
Charleston Gazette	1950 +	WvC

Marshall County

Moundsville Daily Echo	1976	WvMo

Ohio County

Wheeling newspapers	1839 +	WvW

Roane County

Times Record	1913–1975	WvSpCL
	1970 +	WvSpCL

Wood County

Parkersburg News	1972 +	WvSpCL

WISCONSIN

Brown County

DePere News	1871–1883	MiLivWF
Green Bay Advocate	1870–1880	MiLivWF

Jefferson County

Jefferson County newspapers	1853–1879	WWeaJ

Kenosha County

Kenosha newspapers	1845–1945	WKenHi

La Crosse County

Early La Crosse newspapers, including one in German	Ca. 1853–Early 1900's	WLac

Marathon County

Wausau Daily Herald	1965 +	WWsPL

Milwaukee County

**Milwaukee Journal*	No dates given	WMMus
Milwaukee Sentinel	No dates given	WMMus

Racine County

Racine Journal Times	No dates given	WRac

Waukesha County

   Waukesha County newspapers   1863–1881   WWeaJ

Winnebago County

   Oshkosh Daily Northwestern   1868–1977   WOshM

WYOMING

Albany County

   Laramie newspapers   1904–1940   WyLarM

Carbon County

   Grand Encampment Herald   1898–1912   WyEncM

   The Platte Valley Lyre   1883–1903   WyEncM

Natrona County

   Tribune   Pre-1967   WyCaC
               1967 +   WyCaC

Sheridan County

   Sheridan Press   1950 +   WyShS

Sweetwater County

   Green River Star   1970–1977   WyGrM

   Rock Springs Rocket-Miner   1970–1977   WyGrM

FOREIGN NEWSPAPERS

CUBA

The Havana Post	24 March 1912	AMobM

GREAT BRITAIN

The Illustrated London News	23 January 1858; 13, 20, 27 July, 10, 17, 24, 31 August, 7, 14, 21, 28 September, 5, 12, 19, 26 October, 2, 9, 16, 30 (2) November, 7, 14, 21, 28 December 1861; 2 July 1864 (Reprint)	AMobM
The London Chronicle	16–18 March 1870	AMobM
The London Chronicle, or Universal Evening Post	6–9 November 1762	AMobM
The (London) Daily Telegraph	11, 12 May 1926	AMobM
The (London) Flying Post, or Post-Master	24–26 September 1717	AMobM
The London Gazette	5–9, 12–16 January 1720; 4–8 October 1768	AMobM
(London) *Lloyd's Evening Post and British Chronicle*	4–6 January 1762	AMobM

REPOSITORY LOCATIONS

AAnn

Public Library
P. O. Box 308
Anniston, AL 36202

Indexed: General information on Calhoun County area, biography, etc.

I: No charge
C: $.15

ABrJJ   *

John P. Johnston
253 Nassau Street
Brundidge, AL 36010

Indexed: No systematic indexing.
Primarily obituaries and biographical notes—abstracts generally covering persons born before 1849.

I: $5.00 an hour for research, including checking newspaper obituaries, etc. Mr. Johnston is a teacher and can research only during holidays and summer vacation.

The following newspapers are in the Probate Office vault in Troy, AL 36081: *Troy Messenger,* from about 1870 to the present (publication began in 1866); *Troy Enquirer,* 1875–1892; *Troy Herald,* from 1904 until publication ceased; *The Troy Democrat,* 1896 (a few copies); *The Jeffersonian* (a few issues); *The Brundidge News,*

1893–1927; *The Brundidge Sentinel*, from 1928 until publication ceased (a few copies); *Brundidge Banner*, from 1962 to the present (except for a short period of time when publication was interrupted).

All newspapers mentioned have been bound, but may be in poor condition. Bound copies of the *Brundidge Banner* from 1970 to the present are also at the Brundidge Public Library.

Many of these newspapers may have been microfilmed by the Alabama Department of Archives and History, Montgomery, AL 36104.

ACeSU   *

Stewart University System
P. O. Box 295
Centre, AL 35960

Indexed: Marriages, deaths, and other historical notices.
               Genealogical information.

I: No charge
C: $.25

Publication of all newspapers listed has been discontinued.

ADeD

The Decatur Daily
201 First Avenue, S. E.
Decatur, AL 35601

Indexed: All local news, except sports and society.

I: No charge
C: $.10

ADeW

Wheeler Basin Regional Library
P. O. Box 1766
Decatur, AL 35602

Indexed: Local history, Alabama authors, Alabama folk arts.
The Decatur Daily indexed irregularly from 1970–
1976, regularly from 1976.

I: No charge
C: $.15

ALoaLHi

Museum Library
Lee County Historical Society
Alabama at 14
Loachapoka, AL 36865

Indexed: Clipping file.
All historical data pertinent to area.

I: Depends on time and help available. No paid employees
for this purpose.
C: Cost and travel time to Auburn.

AM

Reference Department
Montgomery Public Library
445 South Lawrence Street
Montgomery, AL 36104

Indexed: *Montgomery Advertiser* is indexed on an irregular
basis, usually the Sunday issues.
History, biography and government, for Montgomery
and Alabama.
Miscellaneous subjects.

I: No charge
C: $.10; $.25 from microfilm.

AMob

Mobile Public Library
Mobile, AL 36602

Indexed: Clipping file.
Mobile Press and *Mobile Register* are clipped on 600
Mobile and 600 Alabama subjects, for reference use in the library.
Alabama and Mobile biography, and other subjects
pertaining to Mobile area history.
No obituaries.

I: No charge
C: $.10

AMobHi

Historic Mobile Preservation Society Headquarters
1005 Government Street
Mobile, AL 36604

Indexed: Clipping file.
All subjects of historic, business, or social importance,
on Mobile or Mobilians.

I: $2.50 per item.
C: The Society has no equipment for photocopying.

AMobM

Museum of the City of Mobile
355 Government Street
Mobile, AL 36602

Indexed: Items pertaining to Mobile directly or indirectly.

I: No charge
C: $.10

The (Georgetown) *Federal Republican and Commercial Gazette*, 24 May 1813, was listed but not identified by state.

AU

Reference Office — Room 202
Amelia Gale Gorgas Library
Box S
University, AL 35486

Indexed: From *Tuscaloosa News*, West Alabama news only, not including sports and social events.
From *Birmingham News*, Alabama news.

I: No charge
C: $.10 per sheet, in Southeast. Outside that area, there is a minimum charge of $1.00.
ILL: Microfilm

AkA

Loussac Public Library
427 F Street
Anchorage, AK 99501

Indexed: Clipping file, in 97 loose leaf notebooks.
            Subjects range from aviation (Alaskan) to religion, including history (both Alaskan and Anchorage)—people, towns, pioneers, fishing, native claims, natives, art, earthquake, crime, fisheries, etc.

I: No charge
C: $.15
ILL: Microfilm

AkKTHi

Tongass Historical Society Museum
629 Dock Street
Ketchikan, AK 99901

Indexed: Clipping files, by subject.
             Some items earlier than 1970; 1970–1977, irregularly.
             Local industry, biography, obituaries, organizations,
activities, state items, incidents, court cases.

I: No charge, if item easily located. No staff time for in-depth
        search or research. Searcher may be hired at $5.00 an
        hour.
C: $.10
ILL: Microfilm, from the Alaska State Library, Pouch G,
        Juneau, AK 99811.

State index presently being developed does not include Ketchikan
newspapers.

AkKeHi

Kenai Historical Society, Inc.
Fort Kenai Museum
P. O. Box 1348
Kenai, AK 99611

Indexed: Clipping file—miscellaneous, unorganized.
             Miscellaneous subjects—largely community activities
and events.

I: No charge
C: $.15 and up, according to size

AkKoHi

Kodiak Historical Society
Box 61
Kodiak, AK 99615

C: Current Xerox fees.

Papers saved; on microfilm.

ArBerC

Carroll County Heritage Center
P. O. Box 249
Old 1880 Carroll County Courthouse
Berryville, AR 72616

Indexed: Indexing in progress; files being established.
Local history and genealogy.

I: No charge, for self-search; small fee, if staff searches the
index.
C: $.25

Heritage Center, a county historical museum and library, is being
established. The library will consist of local county history and
geneaology.

AzFM

Museum of Northern Arizona Library
Route 4, Box 720
Flagstaff, AZ 86001

Indexed: Subjective.
          Arizona Daily Sun is clipped.

I: No charge
C: $.10

AzFU

Special Collections
Northern Arizona University Library
C. U. Box 6022
Flagstaff, AZ 86011

Indexed: All Arizona-related information, including births,
          deaths, marriages, and information by subject.

I: No charge
C: $.15 inter-library loan for photocopying from newspaper.
ILL: Microfilm

Arizona Champion-Coconino Sun index available for purchase on
microfilm, fall, 1977. First volume of *Arizona Daily Sun* index
available for copying, late spring, 1978.

AzNPHi

Pimeria Alta Historical Society Museum
701 Grand Avenue
Second Floor, Civic Building
Nogales, AZ 85621

Indexed: Clippings.
          Deaths, biographies, place names, street names, wed-
dings, trips made by Society, facts about the country.

C: None available.

AzPh

Arizona Room
Phoenix Public Library
12 East McDowell Road
Phoenix, AZ 85004

Indexed: Clipping file.
Arizona Republic index is incomplete.
Phoenix Gazette is clipped from approximately 1952 to 1971; some issues clipped to date.

Deaths, biographies, place names, government agencies, general information, etc. There are many subject headings.

I: No charge
C: $.10, up to legal-size.

Special File: McClintock Papers—12 drawers, with alphabetical subject headings. McClintock was newspaper editor and state historian, active in Arizona from 1885–1934.

AzPrSH

Sharlot Hall Museum
415 West Gurley
Prescott, AZ 86301

Indexed: Partial index for *Arizona Journal-Miner.*
Obituaries, biographies, general interest articles.

I: No charge
C: $.20, Xerox.

CAna

Mother Colony History Room
Anaheim Public Library

500 West Broadway
Anaheim, CA 92805

Indexed: Clipping file.
Place names, city departments, deaths, biographical
material, schools, businesses, Anaheim-oriented organizations,
and Orange County government and elections.

I: No charge
C: $.10

CB

Reference Department
Berkeley Public Library
Shattuck and Kittredge Streets
Berkeley, CA 94701

Indexed: Clipping file.
The city's business and government affairs; issues in
California unlikely to be indexed elsewhere.

I: No charge
C: No charge
ILL: Hard copies

CCarm

Harrison Memorial Library
Nixon Local History File Index
Post Box 800
Carmel, CA 93921

Indexed: Events of interest pertaining to local history.
Local places.
Names (obituaries)—authors, artists, local and famous
people.

I: No charge
C: $.10

CFl

Fullerton Public Library
353 West Commonwealth Avenue
Fullerton, CA 92632

Indexed: Fullerton pioneers, notable; Fullerton government,
elections; Fullerton news of community-wide interest.

I: No charge
C: $.10, self-service.

CFrA

Local History Collection
Fremont Library
Alameda County Library System
39770 Paseo Padre Parkway
Fremont, CA 94538

Indexed: Clipping file.
Fremont, Newark, Union City news.
Biographical information on local persons, local places
and local news and events—city council, schools, city planning,
etc.

I: No charge
C: $.10

CLU-URL

Special Collections
University Research Library
University of California
Los Angeles, CA 90024

Indexed: 6,000 catalog cards.
Local events in Los Angeles and southern California.
Advertisements, public notices, literary contributions
by local authors, and editorial comment on the local, state, na-

tional and international levels. Local happenings of whatever nature.

Special attention is paid to personal names on the Los Angeles and southern California scene.

Excluded are national and international news presented without editorial commentary; state news consisting of clips from other newspapers concerning events unrelated to Los Angeles, and presented without editorial commentary; literary materials not produced by local authors; sayings; commonplace facts.

I: No charge for reference service up to fifteen minutes.
C: Prices available through Library Photographic Service, Powell Library Building, UCLA, Los Angeles, CA 90024.

CLob

Long Beach Public Library
101 Pacific Avenue
Long Beach, CA 90802

Indexed: This is a hand-done index to articles about Long Beach which seem significant. Therefore, most activities of clubs, local sports, and crimes, for instance, are not included. Biography, information on port, oil, or government would be the type of article clipped.

I: No charge
C: $.10

CMS

Stanislaus County Library
1402 "Eye" Street
Modesto, CA 95354

Indexed: All local events.
Government meetings.
Biographical information.

I: No charge
C: $.10
ILL: Microfilm

CMary

California Room
Yuba County Library
303 Second Street
Marysville, CA 95901

Indexed: Mr. Earl Ramey has indexed the newspapers from
early 1900 to 1944, plus indexing several books on
local history. His index cards are housed at the Yuba County Library.
City Council minutes, general information in newspapers, weddings, deaths, business deals, local history in general.

I: $5.00 an hour, if someone is hired to check the index; no
charge, if patron comes into the library.
C: $.10, photocopy; $.15, from microfilm.
ILL: Most of the Yuba County Library material from the
California Room does not circulate. Microfilm of the
Marysville newspapers may be borrowed by a local library
from the California State Library, Library-Courts Building,
P. O. Box 2037, Sacramento, CA 95809.

The microfilmed indexes may be available from Library Micro-
films, 737 Loma Verde, Palo Alto, CA 94303.

CMerC

Merced County Library
2100 O Street
Merced, CA 95301

Indexed: Any and all Merced County events and names.

I: No charge
C: $.10

CPlhC

Local History Vertical File—Californiana
Vault Collection—Central Library
Contra Costa County Library
1750 Oak Park Boulevard
Pleasant Hill, CA 94523

Indexed: Extensive clipping files.
Newspapers from about 1935 to 1968 clipped only
sparsely.
Detailed clipping from 1968 to the present.
Place names, biographies, subjects of special tempo-
rary interest, county officials, historic landmarks, industry.

I: No charge for search up to one hour.
C: $.10
ILL: Microfilm

CRiv

Riverside Public Library
P. O. Box 468
3581 Seventh Street
Riverside, CA 92502

Indexed: Local history events by subject, place names, some
personal names.
Coverage varies widely at various times, corresponding to available staff time; virtually nothing from the 1920's and
1930's.

I: No charge, but staff time is limited.
C: $.10, from print; $.15, from microfilm.

CSadH   *

Calaveras Heritage Council
P. O. Box 1281
San Andreas, CA 95249

Indexed: Not complete volumes.

All "official" county newspapers that were received from the County Archives.

Deaths, biographies, place names, marriages and obituaries.

Business, doctors, dentists, fraternal organizations, election results, stage routes, sheriff's business (i.e. Black Bart's stories).

C: $.50
ILL: Microfilm

Bibliography will be available.
Publishing of the indexes is anticipated.

CSj

San Jose Public Library
180 West San Carlos Street
San Jose, CA 95113

Indexed: Two departments have clipping files; the California Room and the Reference Department. Files consist of newspaper clippings and also magazine clippings, brochures, flyers, etc. Clippings are in envelopes, arranged by subject, and located by using a card file kept up to date by each department.

The California Room has clippings of historical and local interest—people, places, events, etc. These are divided into four geographical areas—San Jose, Santa Clara County, San Francisco and California.

The Reference Department file is mostly of current topical interest and broad in coverage and scope.

I: No charge
C: $.10
ILL: No, but the library has microfilm of the *San Jose Mercury* from 1862 to the present, and the *San Francisco Chronicle* from 1953 to the present.

CSmatT   *

The Times
1080 South Amphlett Boulevard
P. O. Box 5400
San Mateo, CA 94402

Indexed: Clipping file. Articles are mounted on paper slips,
              dated and filed in chronological order by name or sub-
ject.
              All San Mateo County news, California State Legisla-
ture news and some national news, i.e. social security, veterans'
information.

I: No charge, for one item. File is available to researchers.
C: $.15, plus tax.

Newspaper is on microfilm, from 1889 to the present.

CStr

Sonoma County Library
Third and E Streets
Santa Rosa, CA 95404

Indexed: Local news of historical interest, including biog-
              raphies.
              For *Press Democrat*, very few pre-1958 clippings.
              For *Petaluma Argus Courier*, some clippings of histor-
ical interest.

I: No charge
C: Ten pages free, then $.10 per page.
ILL: Microfilm

CU-A

Reference Department
Shields Library

UC Davis
Davis, CA 95616

Indexed: Clipping file. Clippings kept for currency, then dis-
carded, when superseded by indexes.
Topics of high popular interest, usually controversial.
Try to keep current to compensate for indexing lag.
Filed under popular word, for easy access.

I: No charge, but include SASE.
C: No charge for short items. For a whole file, or several
clippings, $.15 per exposure. Include SASE.

CU-BANC

University Archives
The Bancroft Library
University of California
Berkeley, CA 94720

Indexed: Card index.
All University news. National and international news
reports are excluded.
The *Daily Californian,* 1929 to the present, is indexed
in the General Library of the University.

I: No charge. Individual index cards may be Xeroxed at $.10
per five or six cards.
C: Rates are established by the Library Photographic Service.

CoC

Pikes Peak Regional Library District
P. O. Box 1579
Colorado Springs, CO 80901

Indexed: Complete indexing, including deaths.
            National news is excluded.
            Library of Congress subject headings.

I: No charge
C: $.10, from hard copy; $.25, from microfilm. No charge for
        first $1.00.
ILL: Microfilm

CoDuF

Southwest Room
Fort Lewis College
College Heights
Durango, CO 81301

Indexed: Local material and Southwest (Colorado, Utah,
            Arizona, and New Mexico).

I: $1.00
C: $.15

CoGj

Mesa County Public Library
530 Grand Avenue
Grand Junction, CO 81501

Indexed: Clipping file.
            Dates are sporadic. File was probably started around
1950 and only added to as staff time permitted. Some items
added to file pre-date that. A more consistent attempt at clipping
started around 1972, for Colorado history and local history.
            Obituary file started in 1976.
            Biographies.

C: $.10 per page, plus $1.00 handling and postage.

CoGjM

Mesa College Library
Grand Junction, CO 81501

Indexed: Clipping file.
         Only the subject of Mesa College.

I: No charge
C: $.10

CoLw

Villa Regional Library
455 South Pierce Street
Lakewood, CO 80226

Indexed: Most general topics. Subject list available on request.

I: No charge
C: $.10

Guide to Colorado Newspapers has much valuable information.

CoStN

Learning Resource Center
Northeastern Junior College
Sterling, CO 80751

Indexed: Any well-informed article, from abortion to Zanzibar.

I: No charge
C: $.10

CtHSD

Nook Farm Research Library
The Stowe-Day Foundation
77 Forest Street
Hartford, CT 06105

Indexed: Miscellaneous clippings, as they relate to nineteenth
        century Hartford, Mark Twain, the Beecher family
and Nook Farm residents, Hartford.

I: No charge, currently
C: $.10
ILL: Hard copies, if duplicates.

DAAUW

Library
AAUW Educational Foundation, Inc.
2401 Virginia Avenue, N. W.
Washington, DC 20037

Indexed: Clippings kept in vertical subject files.
        Subject articles particularly pertaining to women.

C: $.05

DBRE

Association of American Railroads
1920 L Street, N. W.
Washington, DC 20036

Indexed: All aspects of railroading and transportation and other
        economic topics as they affect the railroad industry.

I: No charge
C: No charge

DNGS

National Genealogical Society
1921 Sunderland Place, N. W.
Washington, DC 20036

National Geneaological Society has published three books of
newspaper abstracts. Each book is indexed.

Hardbound Special Publication No. 35: *Genealogical Data from
the New York Post-Boy, 1743–1773* by Kenneth Scott, published
1970, with 143 pages of abstracts, mostly marriages and deaths,
plus a full-name index of 39 pages, $13.25.

Hardbound Special Publication No. 37: *Genealogical Data from
the Pennsylvania Chronicle, 1767–1774* by Kenneth Scott, published 1971. 125 pages of abstracts, mostly marriages and deaths,
plus full-name index of 44 pages, $13.25.

In preparation in 1977: *Marriages and Deaths from the National
Intelligencer, Washington, D.C., 1800–1850*, with a full-name
index to these abstracts included. Approximately 2654 pages,
produced on microfiche, with approximately 500 pages of index.

I: No charge, but include SASE.
C: $.25 per page; $1.00 minimum charge, plus SASE.

National Genealogical Society has no newspapers or microfilmed
newspapers. Books and microfiche publications are for sale
through the above address. 20% discount to members. A
brochure of Special Publications is free, for SASE.

All prices subject to change.

FJU

Swisher Library
Jacksonville University
Jacksonville, FL 32211

Repository—Florida   106

Indexed: State and local politics, government, industries, edu-
          cation, biographies, deaths, place names, history, In-
dians, architecture, art, music, crafts, laws and statutes, etc., fi-
nancial, crime and criminals, drugs, prisons, archaeology, and all
items pertaining to Jacksonville University.
          Indexing is very selective and is determined by the
interests and needs of the students, faculty and administration.

C: $.15

                          FM

          Florida Collection
          Miami-Dade Public Library
          One Biscayne Boulevard
          Miami, FL 33132

Indexed: Fuller clipping after 1960.
          All subjects relating to Florida are clipped, including
biographical items and place name material.

I: No charge, but staff cannot do extensive research by mail.
C: $.20

                         FNiO

          Library
          Okaloosa-Walton Junior College
          Niceville, FL 32578

Indexed: Only newspaper index is *New York Times Index,* lo-
          cated in Periodicals Room.
          Clippings from other newspapers are made selectively
for vertical file, Reference Section; and for scrapbook, Okaloosa-
Walton Junior College Archives.
          For Archives, all Okaloosa-Walton Junior College
items are clipped.
          For Reference Section, subjects of both current and
lasting interest are clipped.

I: No charge, for an individual's checking.
C: $.10
ILL: *New York Times*, on microfilm. Other papers available in hard copy to a limited degree. Library has space to retain only about two months' issues.

FSaHi

Saint Augustine Historical Society
271 Charlotte Street
Saint Augustine, FL 32084

Indexed: Newspaper clippings form a part of the Society's regular files.
Items of historical and genealogical interest dealing with Saint Augustine.

I: No charge
C: $.25

FU

University of Florida Libraries
Department of Reference and Bibliography
Gainesville, FL 32611

Indexed: *Tampa Tribune* clipped for general Florida news only; selective news of statewide interest, including deaths, biographies, place names, etc.
Independent Florida Alligator (student newspaper) indexed for all news reported by student staff. Index on 3″ × 5″ cards.

I: No charge
C: $.05 plus 4% sales tax.

GA

Atlanta Public Library
10 Pryor Street
Atlanta, GA 30303

Indexed: Generally, all subjects encompassing the areas of the
city of Atlanta and of the state of Georgia.

I: No charge
C: $.10
ILL: Hard copies

GAu

Augusta-Richmond County Public Library
902 Greene Street
Augusta, GA 30902

Indexing: Selective indexing of local and Georgia items judged
to be of lasting interest—history, biography, politics
and government, education, etc.

I: No charge
C: $.10 per print, if item is in clipping file; $.25 per print, if
copied from microfilm.

GAuA

Reese Library
Augusta College
2500 Walton Way
Augusta, GA 30904

Indexed: *Augusta Newspaper Digest* is a WPA index, covering
Georgia and Augusta-Richmond County items, mostly
historical and biographical.

Augusta newspapers are clipped for local history materials for vertical file.

I: No charge for search of twenty minutes or less. Longer
       searches are not undertaken.
C: $.10 per page plus postage, for Xerox; $.15 for print from
       microfilm, plus postage.
ILL: No, but exceptions are sometimes made within the state
       for very short periods.

WPA index may also be available at the Augusta Public Library,
Augusta, GA; and University of Georgia Libraries, Athens, GA
30602.

GCai

Roddenbery Memorial Library
North Broad Street
Cairo, GA 31728

Indexed: Historical subjects for local history, Grady County.

C: $.20
ILL: No, but microfilm may be available through University of
       Georgia Libraries, Athens, GA 30602.

GD

Maud M. Burrus Library
215 Sycamore Street
Decatur, GA 30030

Indexed: Mainly, local history for DeKalb County.

I: Vertical file usage free.
C: $.10

The Atlanta Constitution: A Georgia Index by Microfilming Corporation of America, Glen Rock, NJ 07452. Issued annually since
1971. Library has 1971–1974.

GDanH

Heritage Papers
Danielsville, GA 30633

Georgia Marriages and Deaths, 1763–1820, $14.50.
Georgia Marriages and Deaths, 1820–1830, $20.60.

Georgia items are published in book form. South Carolina and North Carolina items will be published in book form.

Newspapers are at Library of Congress, Washington, DC; American Antiquarian Society, Worcester, MA 01609; Georgia Historical Society, Savannah, GA 31401; University of Georgia Libraries, Athens, GA 30602; Georgia Judicial Library; Georgia Department of Archives and History, Atlanta, GA 30334; North Carolina Office of Archives and History, Raleigh, NC 27611; Charleston Library Society, Charleston, SC 29401; South Caroliniana Library, University of South Carolina, Columbia, SC 29208. Scattered issues are elsewhere.

GMarC

Cobb County Public Library System
Central Library
30 Atlanta Street
Marietta, GA 30060

Indexed: Items clipped from newspapers are kept as vertical file material.
Basic arrangement is by subject. Only material considered to be of exceptional or enduring local interest is clipped and may fall within a variety of subject areas.

C: $.10
ILL: Microfilm, on a very limited basis.

Library has the following newspapers on microfilm; *Marietta Daily Journal*, 1868–1976; *Cobb County Times*, 1916–1968; *New York Times*, 1962–1977; *Atlanta Constitution*, 1971–1976.

HPcL

Leeward Community College Library
96-045 Ala Ike
Pearl City, HI 96782

Indexed: Everything

I: No charge
C: $.10

IAl

Hayner Public Library
401 State Street
Alton, IL 62002

Indexed: Deaths, biographies, place names.
              Accidents, weddings, births, etc.

I: No charge
C: $.10

IFDB   *

Mrs. Doris Ellen Bland
401 Tenth Street, N. W.
Fairfield, IL 62837

Indexed: Births, deaths, marriages, divorces, biographies.

I: SASE

Copies of the newspapers are in the storerooms of the Wayne
County Press.

IMolB

Black Hawk College
LRC — ATTN: Nancy Messenger
6600 34th Avenue
Moline, IL 61265

Indexed: Items of local interest, with relevance to curriculum
              needs.
              An attempt is made to provide current information of
local scope.
              Iowa Quad Cities—Davenport and Bettendorf.
              Illinois Quad Cities—Moline and Rock Island.

I: No charge
C: $.10

ISL

Lincoln Library
326 South 7th Street
Springfield, IL 62701

Indexed: Clipping file.
              Deaths, biographies, place names.
              Any subject of historic value, about Springfield and
Sangamon County. Current material on local government,
churches, clubs, citizens, schools, business, art, music. In short,
anything about Springfield.

I: No charge
C: $.10

Ia

State Library Commission of Iowa
East 12th and Grand Avenue
Des Moines, IA 50319

Indexed: Biographies of Iowans.
               Place names in Iowa.
               Iowa Legislature.
               Broad subject topics, such as poetry in Iowa, art in
Iowa, etc.

I: No charge
C: $.10
ILL: Only photocopy

Ia-HA   *

History and Archives
Library
Historical Building
East 12th and Grand Avenue
Des Moines, IA 50319

Indexed: Six file cabinets.
               Iowa history, biographies, prominent persons in art,
literature, theatre.

I: No charge
C: $.10 a page. Limited service, as staff is small.

Ia-NL   *

Newspaper Library
State Historical Building
East 12th and Grand Avenue
Des Moines, IA 50319

Indexed: Partial index of the *Des Moines Register* and the *Des
               Moines Tribune*. At one time all major newspapers of
Iowa were included in the index. Notes government affairs, significant events, people.
               All materials are indexed. Dates range from approxi-
mately 1850 to the present, for the most complete collections.
Daily and weekly papers that are received are microfilmed about

every two to three years. They are not indexed until after they are filmed, but record is kept of every paper received.

I: No charge
C: $.25, from reader-printer. Loose or bound materials cannot be Xeroxed.

IaAS

Iowa State University Library
Reference Department
Ames, IA 50011

Indexed: 1950–1975 is a card file.
1975 to the present is a computer-produced index.
Local, state, regional news, excluding sports and most obituaries.
Access by place, name of person, and event (average of three descriptors per story).

I: No charge, normally.
C: $.10
ILL: Copies from microfilm.

Index is available by subscription, on a sliding scale, based on library acquisitions budgets. The index is produced on a bi-weekly basis, with quarterly and annual cumulations.

IaCf

Cedar Falls Public Library
524 Main Street
Cedar Falls, IA 50613

Indexed: Almost everything of local interest.

I: No charge, when staff has time.
C: $.10

IaCli

Clinton Public Library
306 Eighth Avenue, South
Clinton, IA 52732

Indexed: Deaths, and local items of current or historical importance.
Indexing progresses slowly and is incomplete.

I: No charge
C: $.25, from reader-printer.
ILL: Microfilm

The local historical society reportedly indexed some of the local
newspapers back to 1856 for a county history.

IaCr

Cedar Rapids Public Library
408 Third Avenue, S. E.
Cedar Rapids, IA 52401

Indexed: Card file.
Cedar Rapids deaths.
Cedar Rapids, Linn County, and Iowa items, selec-
tively.

I: $3.00 an hour for research, plus a basic $1.50 handling fee.
C: $.25, from microfilm reader-printer.

IaCrCH   *

Charlene Hansen
Route #1
Cedar Rapids, IA 52401

Indexed: Deaths

I: $1.00 plus SASE.

IaCrLC   *

Lois W. Cronbaugh
337 18th Street, S. E.
Cedar Rapids, IA 52403

Indexed: Items of genealogical nature.

I: One question, no charge. Charge for further searching depends on time involved.

Volume I   *Abstracted Notes from Mt. Vernon, Linn County, Iowa Newspapers, January 1916 through December 25, 1919.*

Volume II   *Abstracted Notes from Mt. Vernon, Linn County, Iowa Newspapers of January 1922 to July 1924.* Weddings, obituaries, etc., including "Supplement—In Remembrance" and some scrapbook clippings.

Volume III   *Abstracted Notes, Mt. Vernon and Lisbon, Iowa Newspapers, 1922, 1923, 1932–1936.* Supplement burials, Lisbon Cemetery, 1893–1895.

Volume IV   *Abstracted Notes from Mt. Vernon and Lisbon, Iowa Newspapers, 1947–1950.* "Way Back When," 1903–1938.

Volume V   *Abstracted Notes from Mt. Vernon and Lisbon, Iowa Newspapers, January 1920–December 1921, January 1924 through 1926.* St. John's Parish; History of Mt. Vernon; Impressions of Cornell College; Craig Cemetery.

Each volume is $15. The following libraries have copies of these volumes: Iowa State Historical Society Library, Iowa City, IA; Iowa State Library, Des Moines, IA; Public Library of Fort Wayne and Allen County, Fort Wayne, IN.

The original newspapers were destroyed, but microfilm copies are in the Iowa State Library, Des Moines, IA.

IaDm

Public Library of Des Moines
Reference Department
100 Locust
Des Moines, IA 50309

Indexed: 1946 to the present, on 3″ × 5″ cards; mounted clip-
            pings and a printed index cover the 1920's, 1930's and
1940's in much less detail; biographical scrapbook dates to 1900.
            Clipped—biographical articles, articles of historic
interest, pictures, etc.
            Indexed—Des Moines, Polk County, and Iowa infor-
mation. There are not too many personal name entries. Excluded
are society news and most sports.

I: No charge
C: $.10 from hard copy (recent issues only); $.25 from micro-
        film.
ILL: Microfilm, if not in use at the library, i.e. most recent, or
        historical papers, such as those on Pearl Harbor, etc.

IaGG

College Archives
Burling Library
Grinnell College
Grinnell, IA 50112

Indexed: College activities.

I: No charge, for a few items.
C: $.15
ILL: Microfilm

IaHi

State Historical Society of Iowa Library
402 Iowa Avenue
Iowa City, IA 52240

Indexed: Deaths, biographies, place names.
Thousands of clippings, which have not been organized.

ILL: Microfilm

Newspaper collection consists of 2000 volumes and 7000 rolls of microfilm, dating back to 1836. Collection includes some Iowa-published foreign language newspapers.

Newspaper Collection of the State Historical Society of Iowa by L. O. Cheever is available for $.75 (postage paid). It was published in 1969 and is out of date, but a revision is planned.

IaOskW

Wilcox Library
William Penn College
Oskaloosa, IA 52577

Indexed: No index. Some clipping.
Information about William Penn College.

C: $.10

IaWbH   *

Herbert Hoover Presidential Library
West Branch, IA 52358

Indexed: Library has 353 document boxes of Subject Files in
Post-Presidential Subject Files. These files contain correspondence, printed material and clippings, dated 1933–1964.
Library has 450 document boxes of Clipping Files from not only leading newspapers, but also state and county papers, which pertain to Herbert Hoover and his work from 1917 to 1964, arranged in chronological order.
In addition, the library has the following reels of microfilmed un-indexed foreign newspapers: *Herbert Hoover's 1928 Latin*

American Tour, 1 reel; *Herbert Hoover's Trip to Europe, 1938*, 2 reels; and *Herbert Hoover's Famine Survey of South America, 1946*, 1 reel.

I: No charge
C: $.20 by mail, with $2.00 minimum.

IdB

Boise Public Library
715 Capitol Boulevard
Boise, ID 83706

Indexed: Clipping file.
A few clippings from July 1964 through intervening years.

Quite completely clipped from 1973 to the present.
Biography.
Boise history and current news—arranged by subject in Boise file.
Idaho history and current news—arranged by subject in Idaho file.
Library has an index only of the subjects clipped.

C: $.10 per photocopy; $.15 per shot for microfilm—it often takes two or three shots to get one article.

The *Idaho Statesman* is on microfilm from July 1864 to the present, and staff will search it, if patron can give fairly accurate date item may have been in paper.

IdIf

Idaho Falls Public Library
457 Broadway
Idaho Falls, ID 83401

Indexed: Clipping file; varies; generally fairly current. Old clippings sometimes weeded.

Pioneers, local histories, controversial issues, items pertaining to library of region, Idaho towns, Idaho history, reclamation, public lands.

Idaho Falls—history, city facilities and businesses, etc.

I: No charge
C: $.10

IdPI

Periodicals Department
Idaho State University Library
Pocatello, ID 83209

Indexed: Comprehensive index, covering most subjects.

I: Staff does not check the index for patrons.
ILL: Microfilm

IdRR

Ricks College L. R. C.
Rexburg, ID 83440

Indexed: Clipping file.
             Deaths.

I: No charge
C: No charge, up to three pages.

InE

Adult Information Department
Evansville Public Library-Vanderburgh County Public Library

22 S. E. Fifth Street
Evansville, IN 47708

Indexed: Items of local permanent interest, including biog-
             raphies of local citizens.
             Local Evansville papers were previously clipped.
Some items are from as far back as 1915. *Evansville Courier,
Courier and Press,* and *Press* are indexed.

C: $.10

InEM   *

Evansville Museum of Arts and Science
411 S. E. Riverside Drive
Evansville, IN 47713

Indexed: Museum also has some unclipped papers—local and
             from elsewhere, too numerous to list.
             Vanderburgh County history—includes biographical
material, architecture, business, industry, organizations, public
and private facilities, celebrations and other activities, etc.
             Biographical material on artists in the collection.

I: No charge
C: $.10

InElw   *

Elwood Public Library
124 North 16th Street
Elwood, IN 46036

Indexed: Deaths.
             Some marriages, from 1966–1971.

I: No charge. Searches made on basis of time allowed, if staff
        is not busy.
C: $.20 for single copy. For multiple copies, $.20 each for the
        first five and $.10 for each additional copy.
ILL: Microfilm

InIS   *

"Indiana Ancestors"
% The Indianapolis Star
307 North Pennsylvania Street
Indianapolis, IN 46206

Indexed: "Indiana Ancestors" is a genealogy column.
        Indexes cover all surnames that have appeared in the
queries, book notices, responses, reunion notices, and all sur-
names of those who sent in queries, etc.

Indiana Ancestors Index I, 1 July 1973–30 June 1974 is $2.50.
This is an index only.

Indiana Ancestors Index II, 1 July 1974–30 June 1975 is in process of being published. It will include index and all columns.

Indiana Ancestors Index III, 1 July 1975–30 June 1976 is in process
of being published and it will include index and all columns.

Copies of the column are in the possession of the column's editor,
Rebecca Roth; and at the Indiana State Library, Genealogy Divi-
sion, Indianapolis, IN 46204; Public Library of Fort Wayne and
Allen County, Fort Wayne, IN; The Night Owl Library, 9430
Vandergriff Road, Indianapolis, IN 46239.

InNea

New Albany-Floyd County Public Library
180 West Spring Street
New Albany, IN 47150

Indexed: 1970 to the present already indexed. Retrospective
        indexing in progress. Some items for 1974–1976 are
clipped.
        Biographical, businesses, buildings, obituaries.

I: No charge, ordinarily, but return postage is requested.
C: $.10 per page, from a clipping; $.25 per page, from microfilm.

InWinaCL   *

Pulaski County Public Library
121 South Riverside Drive
Winamac, IN 46996

Indexed: Chiefly births, deaths, marriages.
          Card index, presented to the library by the Pulaski
County Genealogical Society.
          The *Pulaski County Journal* is a consolidation of all
newspapers ever published in Winamac. Additional names of
newspapers in this consolidation: *Greenback Journal*, 1878–1883;
Winamac Perfect, 1888–1891; *Winamac Republican*, August
1974–November 1975.

I: Contact library for current policies.
C: Contact library for current policies.
ILL: Microfilm and hard copies available only for in-house use.

K

Kansas State Library
State House—Third Floor
Topeka, KS 66612

Indexed: Card file.
          Mostly Kansas and Kansans.
          Individuals—governors, congressmen, judges, etc.
          State agencies, historical landmarks, etc.

I: No charge
C: $.10 per page, for personal use.

KDcC   *

Cultural Heritage and Arts Center
P. O. Box 1275
1000 Second Avenue
Dodge City, KS 67801

Indexed: Items of historical interest, comments on history and culture of the Old West, art and artists, authors from the Southwest, book reviews.

I: Small service fee.
C: $.10 and $.15 per page.

KEm

Emporia Public Library
118-120 East Sixth Avenue
Emporia, KS 66801

Indexed: Indexed by personal name.

I: No charge
C: $.25 per exposure, with $1.00 minimum.

KWi

Wichita Public Library
225 South Main
Wichita, KS 67202

Indexed: Clipping file.
          Kansas and Wichita news—buildings, public officials, biographies, famous visitors, city and state political issues.

I: No charge

KyOw   *

Owensboro Public Library
450 Griffith Avenue
Owensboro, KY 42301

Indexed: Only information on Owensboro, Daviess County, and surrounding areas.
Includes death notices, subject and biographical index.

I: $1.00
C: $.10 a page, plus $1.00 service charge.

LGra

Serials Area
A. C. Lewis Memorial Library
Grambling State University
Grambling, LA 71245

Indexed: Out-of-state papers listed are indexed. Louisiana papers are clipped.
Biographies, place names, University news items.

I: No charge
C: $.10

LMetJ   *

Jefferson Parish Library Headquarters
Melvil Dewey Drive at North Causeway Boulevard
Metairie, LA 70010

Indexed: All general subjects, plus personal names.
Local, state, national, and international news articles.

I: No charge
C: $.25, from microfilm.

LNPo

Polyanthos
Drawer 51359
New Orleans, LA 70151

Indexed: All genealogical material abstracted.
Bound volume, available spring, 1978, $30.00.

LNaN

Special Collections Division
Watson Memorial Library
Northwestern State University of Louisiana
Natchitoches, LA 71457

Indexed: Biographies, place names, feature stories, local and
state history, parish history, deaths, and anything that
fits vertical file subjects.
250-plus Melrose scrapbooks contain voluminous clippings.

I: No charge
C: $.20
ILL: Microfilm and hard copies.

LSh

Shreve Memorial Library
400 Edwards
Shreveport, LA 71101

Indexed: Feature articles, political and governmental articles,
biographies.

I: No charge
C: $.20, up to legal-size.

LShC

Magale Library
Centenary College
Shreveport, LA 71104

Indexed: Local interest and local figures.

I: No charge
C: $.10
ILL: Microfilm, if replaceable.

LU-E

LeDoux Library
Louisiana State University at Eunice
Eunice, LA 70535

Indexed: Deaths

I: No charge
C: $.10
ILL: Microfilm

MBAt

Boston Athenaeum
10½ Beacon Street
Boston, MA 02108

Indexed: Marriages and deaths for the *Massachusetts Centinel*
and the *Columbian Centinel.*
     For the *Gazette*, deaths, and partial indexing of
births, vocations, and marriages.

I: No charge, but staff cannot check long lists of names.
C: $.25 per page, plus $2.00 for handling and postage.

MGlHi

Cape Ann Historical Association
27 Pleasant Street
Gloucester, MA 01930

Indexed: Not all indexed or filed. Not complete for either
newspaper.
Local obituaries, historical facts, etc.

MHa

Haverhill Public Library
99 Main Street
Haverhill, MA 01830

Indexed: Local history—biography, authors, artists, banks,
business, celebrations, churches, houses, taverns,
labor, labor unions, library, lodges, manufacturers, shoe manufacturers, shoes, monuments, names, natural history, imprints, railroads, rivers, schools, societies.

The same topics are indexed about adjacent towns—
Andover, Boxford, Methuen, Groveland, Georgetown, West
Newbury, Merrimac, Newbury, Newbury Port, Amesbury,
Salisbury—all in Massachusetts.

The same topics are also indexed about Plaistow, Atkinson, Danville, Kensington, Kingston—all in New Hampshire.

I: No charge
C: $.25

There are numerous other papers published locally for a brief
period, including ethnic papers (2 Greek, 2 French, etc.). Many
have been clipped but only for items of local interest, nothing of
national importance. All have been microfilmed. The best index
by subject is of the *Haverhill Evening Gazette.* This indexing was
done by the WPA during the 1930's, but again, only items of
local history. All the other papers listed are either clipped or
sporadically indexed.

MLy

Lynn Public Library
5 North Common Street
Lynn, MA 01902

Indexed: All Lynn newspapers—not completely indexed.
              General indexing, including deaths, biographies, and
place names.

I: No charge, if item is indexed.
C: $.10, if scrapbook item; if microfilm, work done through
       Graphic Microfilm, Waltham, MA. Inquirer must contact
       them directly.

MNBedf

Genealogy Room
Free Public Library
Box C-902
New Bedford, MA 02741

Indexed: Local news and history, obituaries, local features.

I: No charge
C: $.25
ILL: Microfilm

MNoad

North Adams Public Library
Church Street
North Adams, MA 01247

Indexed: For 1844 to 1874, index cards, covering deaths, place
              names, people. This index is at the library.

I: No charge
C: $.25

Staff members at *The Transcript*, in North Adams, MA have reportedly indexed the paper since about 1930. This is not at the library.

MNtS

Swedenborg School of Religion
48 Sargent Street
Newton, MA 02158

Indexed: Clippings only, not filed by location.
Anything about anybody or any event mentioning the New Church, Emmanuel Swedenborg, Swedenborgian Church, General Convention of the New Jerusalem in United States and Canada, etc.

I: Generally no charge.
C: $.08

MSo

Somerville Public Library
Main Branch
Highland Avenue and Walnut Street
Somerville, MA 02143

Indexed: Papers both clipped and indexed.
Separate biography index started 1 June 1934 (notables only).
Only those articles are indexed which pertain to Somerville and which will be of some lasting interest to the community, e.g. community redevelopment, local history, social service agencies.
Sports items and club news items are excluded.

I: No charge
C: $.10

MWalA

American Jewish Historical Society Library
2 Thornton Road
Waltham, MA 02154

Indexed: Places, individuals, institutions—broad subject
categories.

I: No charge
C: $.10
ILL: Microfilm

MdHag

Washington County Free Library
100 South Potomac Street
Hagerstown, MD 21740

Indexed: Clipping file.
           Local history, state information, county information,
deaths (prominent persons), local industries, and library publicity.

I: No charge
C: $.10 a page, in the library; mail requests are absorbed in
       the budget.
ILL: Microfilm, but only by written request, and rolls must be
       insured. Hard copies are also available.

Library has two local newspapers on microfilm: *Morning Herald,*
31 December 1895 to the present; *Daily Mail,* 1 September 1890
to the present.

MdLapC

Learning Resource Center
Charles County Community College

Box 910, Mitchell Road
LaPlata, MD 20646

Indexed: Newspapers have been clipped for articles of lasting
importance, particularly about Maryland.
Mounted articles are in library's vertical file and do
circulate.

I: No charge
C: $.05

MeHi

Maine Historical Society Library
485 Congress Street
Portland, ME 04111

Indexed: No indexes for specific papers. Cited newspapers are
clipped, in scrapbooks, mostly 1880–1920.
Obituaries, biographies and historical articles, clipped
with various scrapbooks, all of which are indexed.

I: No charge, by mail. Free to members in library; $1.00 a
day use fee for non-members.
C: $.25 a page to non-members; $.10 a page to members.

MeMacU

Merrill Library
University of Maine at Machias
Machias, ME 04654

Indexed: The only indexes are purchased.
Bangor Daily News and *Portland Press Herald* are
clipped for alumni news.

C: $.10
ILL: No, but microfilm may be available through the city of
       publication.

Mi

Michigan Unit
Michigan State Library
Box 30007
Lansing, MI 48909

Indexed: Biographies, all subjects relating to Michigan and
             Michigan localities.
             No births, deaths, marriages.
             Occasionally other state papers are indexed; also all
types of ephemera.
             The State Library also holds indexes for newspapers
from the following Michigan cities—Detroit, Coldwater,
Kalamazoo, Three Rivers, Flint, Bay City. Coverage varies.

I: No charge
C: $.10
ILL: Microfilm. Michigan State Library has over 50,000 rolls of
       Michigan newspapers on microfilm. The checklist, cur-
       rently out of print, will be available in 1978.

MiBay

Bay City Branch Library
708 Center Avenue
Bay City, MI 48706

Indexed: From 1935 to 1954, the index is on cards in a catalog;
             from 1955 to the present, the index is published in
book form.

Items pertaining to Bay County, and some things about the rest of Michigan that pertain to the county—legislation, etc.

I: No charge
C: $.10

Five copies of the index are printed, one of which is on file with the Michigan State Library (see Mi).

MiDecCL   *

Van Buren County Library
Webster Memorial Building
200 Phelps Street
Decatur, MI 49045

Indexed: Deaths, local (Van Buren County) interests.

I: No charge
C: $.10
ILL: Microfilm; *Decatur Republican* and *Paw Paw Courier Leader*, only.

MiFd   *

Ferndale Public Library
222 East Nine Mile Road
Ferndale, MI 48220

Indexed: All local newspaper history articles for the *Ferndale Gazette-Times* and the *Daily Tribune* are clipped.
        Some articles are also clipped from the *Detroit News* and *Detroit Free Press*.
        Deaths, biographies, education, schools, buildings, abortion, metric system, Detroit buildings, Michigan history.
        A separate file concerning Ferndale city affairs.
        Vertical file material covers subjects from A to Z.

I: No charge
C: $.15 a page, up to legal-size.

Ferndale Gazette-Times is on microfilm, from 1927 to the present.

MiFliJ   *

Editorial Library
The Flint Journal
200 East First Street
Flint, MI 48502

Indexed: Clipping files from 1935 to the present; microfilm files
from 1898 to the present.
Local people, business, history.

The Library does not provide services to the public. The index is
available for purchase, from the Flint Public Library, Flint, MI
48502. The index covers 1963 to the present.

MiGrSE   *

Sandra Elliott
62 Peony Street, S. W.
Grand Rapids, MI 49508

Indexed: Obituaries.

I: $1.00 per surname.

$3.50 for booklet without index.
$5.50 for booklet with index.

Newspapers are in the home of Sandra Elliott.

MiJoBM   *

Mrs. Barbara McCreight
113 Spruce Drive
Jonesville, MI 49250

Indexed: Marriages and deaths—all items found on those subjects.

I: $5.00 for each surname.
C: $.25 a page, mostly from microfilm.

Mrs. McCreight plans to publish material in 1978.

MiL

Lansing Public Library
401 South Capitol Avenue
Lansing, MI 48914

Indexed: Deaths and biographies of locally prominent or well-known people.
Business births and deaths, local history, and local politics and government.

I: No charge
C: $.10 a page, from clippings; $.25 a quarter page, from microfilm.

MiLivWF   *

Mrs. Wilma A. Foley
19374 Ingram Avenue
Livonia, MI 48152

Indexed: All vital records abstracted and indexed, with additional bride's index. There are approximately 1200 events for each of three volumes, plus the bride's index.

I: $1.00 per event, plus SASE. Money returned if nothing found.

Volume I   *Marriage Abstracted and Indexed from the Green Bay Advocate, 1870–1880,* $10.50 postpaid.

Volume II   *Deaths Abstracted and Indexed from the Green Bay Advocate, 1870–1880,* $8.50 postpaid.

Volume III   *Marriages and Deaths Abstracted and Indexed from the DePere News* by Wilma Foley and Patricia Gee, $12.50 postpaid. Wisconsin kept early vital records, but *only those that were reported.* An estimated 70% were *not* reported. These abstracts are from the *first* 12 years of the *first* newspaper printed in DePere, Brown County, Wisconsin. Alphabetized, with bride's index. Obits contained much genealogical information. Other areas were covered that had connections with Brown County.

All three volumes were compiled by Wilma A. Foley and Patricia Gee, and they may be purchased from Mrs. Foley. Each of these copyrighted books is a limited edition of 100 copies.

The newspapers are on microfilm in the Newspaper Section of the State Historical Society of Wisconsin Library, Madison, WI 53706.

MiPh

Port Huron Public Library
St. Clair County Library System
Port Huron, MI 48060

Indexed: Clipping file.
                  Items of state and local interest and some of national
interest.
                  Items of city and county interest are clipped,
mounted, and filed in the library's historical collection room.
                  Local and county obituaries are clipped. Small weekly
papers of the county are clipped for news and obituaries.

I: No charge
C: $.20
ILL: Microfilm. Library has *Port Huron Times Herald* on micro-
         film for 1844, 1845, and from 1850 to the present.

Miscs   *

Saint Clair Shores Public Library
22500 Eleven Mile Road
Saint Clair Shores, MI 48081

Indexed: Clipping file.
Materials relating to the city of Saint Clair Shores,
Michigan—city government, law enforcement, history, recreation,
organizations, education, etc.

I: No charge
C: $.10

MiWy

Local History Collection
Bacon Memorial Public Library
45 Vinewood
Wyandotte, MI 48192

Indexed: From 1880 to around 1964, indexed and selectively
clipped—clippings in scrapbooks.
1960 to June 1975, clipped and arranged by subject in
envelopes.
From June 1975, index is maintained on 3″ × 5″
cards, and is divided into parts—personal names and subjects. A
notation is made when a photograph accompanies an article.
Prior to June 1975, obituaries, biographies, place
names and subjects were indexed.
Currently, the index serves as a guide to newspaper
articles of interest and importance about Wyandotte people,
places, and things.
Vital statistics columns are omitted, but obituaries are
included.
Most advertisements, routine sports events, and non-
news items about such things as hobbies and homemaking are not
indexed.

I: No charge, for reasonable requests.
C: $.10
ILL: No, but Michigan State Library will interlibrary loan
        copies (see Mi).

MnU-IA

Immigration History Research Center
University of Minnesota
826 Berry Street
Saint Paul, MN 55114

Indexed: All subjects.
         Indexing in progress for newspaper in the Carpatho-
Ruthenian language.

I: No charge
C: $.10
ILL: Microfilm, from the University of Pittsburgh Library.

List of publications available. The Center's purpose is to aid and
encourage research into migrations of people from Eastern,
Southern and Central Europe and the Middle East, and to encourage examination of the sub-societies they established in
America.

MoCg

Cape Girardeau Public Library
Court House Park
Cape Girardeau, MO 63701

Indexed: Obituaries, topics of general interest, e.g. Mississippi
         River, law enforcement, handicapped, courts, chil-
dren, business, arts, crafts, etc.

I: No charge

C: $.10 or $.15, depending on the size of the copy.

A limited number of copies are printed of each year's index and are sold for $1.00. Most are purchased by local community organizations.

MoExGS

Excelsior Springs Genealogical Society
Box 601
Excelsior Springs, MO 64024

ILL: Microfilm, possibly.

MoGSS   *

Saline Sentiments
Route 1, Box 16
Gilliam, MO 65330

Indexed: Obituaries, death notices, newsworthy items, printed verbatim from old newspapers, some dating to 1870's. These concern Saline County and other Missouri residents of the past. Includes names, place, and date of newspaper.

I: Will search holdings on obituaries only. No personal research. Minimum order, $1.00.

C: Order by full name of deceased, with date and place of demise, when possible, and name of spouse or parents, if known. Each article or page, $.35, or 3 articles or pages, $1.00, or order volumes described below.

The following volumes are in limited supply. All are duplicated, stapled, with soft covers:

Volume I   Over 2000 full names, with month and year, on which a newsworthy article is available. Certificate for two articles free. $3.00.

Volume II   Over 1300 names, same information as above, plus 10 pages of marriages and items of interest from the *Gilliam Globe* for 1918–1925. $3.50.

Volume III   Over 2000 names, same as above. $3.00.

Volume IV   Over 1500 names, same as above, plus 13 pages of marriages, Book C, Saline County. $3.00.

MoJcT

Thomas Jefferson Library
214 Adams Street
Jefferson City, MO 65101

Indexed: Limited indexing began in early 1966, but major indexing began in 1968 and has continued.
Local, county, and state politics and government news.
Prominent people in community and government.
Local, county, and state agencies.
Affairs of broad interest to community and state.
Historical items.
Community organizations.

I: No charge
C: $.10, up to legal-size, from microfilm.

MoLaSS   *

Sarah Sisson
Route #1, Box 404
Lawson, MO 64062

Indexed: Deaths, births, school reports, parties, and other items of genealogical interest.

Index is in book form. Volume I is $5.50.

The newspapers are in the possession of Sarah Sisson.

MoSLS   *

Lois Stanley
8740 Nashville
Saint Louis, MO 63117

Indexed: Deaths, estates, divorces, separations, missing per-
              sons, bankruptcies, notice of trust sales (naming both
husband and wife).
              When every possible newspaper has been indexed for
the subjects listed, the researchers plan to go back and extract
other information on topics such as runaway slaves, indentured
servants, names in the proceedings of the Legislature, etc.
              Marriage records which did not appear in civil records
are also being abstracted from the newspapers and will be published.

I: All entries for one surname, $2.00 plus SASE. $1.00 will
        be refunded, if the name is not found.
C: $.25, from bound volumes.
ILL: Microfilm from the State Historical Society of Missouri,
        Columbia, MO 65201; or Missouri Historical Society Li-
        brary, Saint Louis, MO 63112. A few of the newspapers
        indexed may not be available and copies may be found in
        repositories in the cities where they were printed. Except
        for the long run of the *Gazette-Republican,* there are
        rarely more than a few years of any one newspaper avail-
        able. Generally, the newspapers cover most of the state at
        one time or another, but not the whole state the whole
        time.

MoSavHi

Andrew County Historical Society
Savannah, MO 64485

Indexed: Birth records—only parents' names, dates, sex of
              child.
              Obituaries—complete from 1876 to 1920; rest very
sketchy; many years missing.

C: $1.00 plus SASE, to copy obituary from microfilm, if available.

Microfilmed newspapers are at Missouri State Historical Society, Columbia, MO 65201; *Savannah Reporter*, Savannah, MO 64485.

MoSp

Springfield-Greene County Library
M. P. O. Box 737
397 East Central
Springfield, MO 65801

Indexed: Biographical, local government, schools, crimes, business organizations, associations.
Local history, for all Southwest Missouri.

I: In general, search service is not available.
C: $.10 per page; $1.00 minimum.

MoSpLW   *

"Ozark Genealogy"
Lena Wills
635 East Bennett
Springfield, MO 65807

Indexed: Queries to weekly genealogy column.

I: Probably $1.00 to $2.00
C: Cost of having records Xeroxed.

Lena Wills has complete file of the columns.

MsGW

Washington County Library System
341 Main
Greenville, MS 38701

Indexed: Local history, biographies of local importance.

I: No charge, if in-depth research is not involved.
C: $.10

MsHos

Marshall County Library
207 Van Dorn Avenue
Holly Springs, MS 38635

Indexed: Local history of Holly Springs and Marshall County,
            which includes Holly Springs Garden Club Pilgrimage
each year in April.
            Biographies, deaths.
            Marshall Messenger indexed for approximately five
years.

I: No charge, for small number of searches.
C: $.10

Bound volumes of the *South Reporter*, from early 1880's to the
present, are stored in the Chancery Clerk's Office, Marshall County
Courthouse, Holly Springs, MS 38635.

MsV

Vicksburg-Warren County Library
P. O. Box 511
Vicksburg, MS 39180

Indexed: Clipping file.
            News articles, people, places, organizations, photos.

I: No charge
C: $.15
ILL: Microfilm

MtBilE

Eastern Montana College Library
Billings, MT 59101

Indexed: The 1930–1949 index is at the library.
The 1976 index is a joint project with the Billings
Public Library. This service, which is just beginning, is about
$400 a year, from the Billings Public Library.
Montana history, Montana current interest items, and
Eastern Montana College items.

C: $.10
ILL: Microfilm

MtG

Glendive Public Library
Box 1329
Glendive, MT 59330

Indexed: Only clippings of historical interest or those that
might contain up-to-date information on topics of current interest, such as strip mining.

I: No charge
C: $.10

MtHi

Montana Historical Society
225 North Roberts
Helena, MT 59601

Indexed: Since the mid-1870's, there has been a random attempt to clip or index assorted Montana newspapers.
No one paper has been indexed or clipped for a full year.
Subjects clipped or indexed vary. They include biographical information, obituaries, and historical events or articles.

I: No charge to check either the index or the vertical clip-
        ping file.
C: $.20 per page, with $1.00 minimum.
ILL: Microfilm

MtU

University of Montana
Missoula, MT 59812

Indexed: Biographies, all information on Montana.
            Deaths, as of 1976.

I: Currently, no charge.
C: Fee
ILL: Microfilm

NAlI

McKinney Library
Albany Institute of History and Art
125 Washington Avenue
Albany, NY 12210

Indexed: Biographies, events, buildings, and historical articles
            on Albany area.

C: $.15

NAuHi

County Historian Office
County Office Building
Auburn, NY 13021

Indexed: Obituaries and outstanding events.

I: $1.00
C: $.50

NBi

Information Service
Binghamton Public Library
78 Exchange Street
Binghamton, NY 13901

Indexed: Clipping file and pamphlet file; no index.
               Clipped—local government, biographies, deaths, li-
brary, local history.

C: Clippings may be Xeroxed at $.10 a page.

NBu

Buffalo and Erie County Public Library
History Department
Lafayette Square
Buffalo, NY 14203

Indexed: A very selective file and not a complete index. It is
               primarily a local history file.
               Deaths, biographies, place names for city and suburbs
in Erie and neighboring counties, schools, businesses, cultural institutions, clubs, historical figures or sites, sports, crime and criminals, famous visitors.

I: Currently, no searching for mail requests, as there is no
        staff for this purpose.
C: $.10
ILL: Some microfilm duplicates.

The Buffalo and Erie County Historical Society, 25 Nottingham
Court, Buffalo, NY 14216 has indexes of two Buffalo newspapers
back to the early nineteenth century.

NEh

Long Island Collection
East Hampton Free Library
159 Main Street
East Hampton, NY 11937

Indexed: Some issues missing in each title.
Deaths, marriages, feature articles, front page.

I: No charge
C: Varies

NEmNHi   *

Nassau County Museum Reference Library
Eisenhower Park
East Meadow, NY 11554

Indexed: Clippings.
Nassau County history, obituaries of county residents,
biographical items of county residents.

I: No charge
C: $.25
ILL: Microfilm, limited to two rolls at a time.

NGHi   *

Archives of the Geneva Historical Society
543 South Main Street
Geneva, NY 14456

Indexed: Marriages and deaths.
Subjects such as religion, education, fires, local happenings, transportation, etc. have been indexed up to 1880; all
pertaining to Geneva only and not complete for all years.

I: No charge
C: $.10

NHerkCHi

Herkimer County Historical Society
400 North Main Street
Herkimer, NY 13350

Indexed: Deaths, births, marriages, some biographies.

I: Donation
C: $.20

NHuHi

Library
Huntington Historical Society
New York Avenue and High Street
P. O. Box 506
Huntington, NY 11743

Indexed: The *Long Islander,* 1839–1845—everything, excluding
marriages and deaths, relevant to the history of Huntington Township as a geographical area of the United States,
situated on Long Island, New York.

C: Costs vary.

Microfilm available for purchase at $60.00 a reel, 1839–1936. In-
dexes for sale at $4.00 a volume.

NNSIHi

Staten Island Historical Society
Richmondtown
Staten Island, NY 10306

Indexed: Important deaths, biographies, local history, etc.

I: No charge
C: $.10

NNia

Local History Department
Niagara Falls Public Library
1425 Main Street
Niagara Falls, NY 14305

Indexed: All local topics—births, deaths, etc.

I: No charge
C: $.10

NOcaS

Emma King Library
The Shaker Museum
Old Chatham, NY 12136

Indexed: Items dealing with the Shakers.

I: No charge
C: $.20 to $.25

NOg

Ogdensburg Public Library
312 Washington Street
Ogdensburg, NY 13669

Indexed: Partial index to local events for Ogdensburg.
Biographies and special events.

I: Minimum of $2.00.

NR

Rochester Public Library
115 South Avenue
Rochester, NY 14604

Indexed: Although 18 newspapers were indexed for the period
            1818–1897, the index is not inclusive of all Rochester
papers published during that period.

Marriages, obituaries, business and governmental appointments, crimes and criminal cases, accidents, church dedications, election results, etc.

I: No charge, but staff cannot do extensive research.
C: $.10

The index is for sale. Write for the current price.

NRGR   *

Library
Gannett Rochester Newspapers
55 Exchange Street
Rochester, NY 14614

Indexed: Local news by subject and personal names.
            Regional news (ten counties) by subject.
            State government news by subject.
            Wire news on national and international level is not
clipped.

I: No charge
C: $.25 per letter-size sheet; $2.00 per page.

NRomHi   *

Rome Historical Society
113 West Court Street
Rome, NY 13440

Indexed: In general, the total newspaper.

I: $5.00 per hour; members free.
C: $.15 per copy, for Xerox, plus $1.00 handling, for up to 10
       copies.

NSm

Smithtown Library
1 North Country Road
Smithtown, NY 11787

Indexed: Clipping file—vertical file index.
Local news, biographies, political, economic, cultural, government, items of local import, and historical articles.

I: No charge
C: $.10

NSyCM   *

Canal Museum
Weighlock Building
Erie Boulevard, East
Syracuse, NY 13202

Indexed: Articles concerning the Canal Museum, the Old Erie
Canal State Park, and canals in general.

I: No charge
C: $.10

NT

Troy Public Library
100 Second Street
Troy, NY 12180

Indexed: Marriage and obituary notices.

I: No charge
C: $.10 for Xerox copy; $.20 from microfilm.
ILL: Microfilm

NbB

Beatrice Public Library
Beatrice, NE 68310

Indexed: The library does not have an index, but does have access to the *Beatrice Daily Sun* clipping files, which are kept for ten years.

NbH

Hastings Public Library
Fourth and Denver
P. O. Box 849
Hastings, NE 68901

Indexed: Card index and bound volume, *Hastings, Nebraska Newspaper Index, 1872–1938.*
Numerous subject headings, from Accidents to Weddings.

I: No charge
C: $.10

NbKS

Kearney State College Library
Kearney, NE 68847

Indexed: Nebraska items.

I: No charge
C: $.10

NbO

Omaha Public Library
215 South 15th
Omaha, NE 68102

Indexed: Clipping file.

Indexed more thoroughly from the late 1930's, but there are some cards, etc. for dates much farther back.

Businesses, government, etc. that relate to Nebraska or Omaha.

C: $3.00 minimum, which includes the first five pages of copies; $.10 per copy thereafter.

ILL: Microfilm

The library has newspapers dating back to 1857.

NbOPC   *

Universal Press Clipping Bureau
403 Farnam Building
Omaha, NE 68102

Indexed: All material dealing with Peru State College and Board of Trustees.

I: No charge
C: $.05

NcDur

Durham County Public Library
P. O. Box 3809
Durham, NC 27702

Indexed: No index. Newspapers have been clipped sparingly.

Material on the library, Durham biographies, material on local history and places.

ILL: Microfilm

The library has the *Durham Morning Herald* from January 1944 to date, and the *Durham Sun* from June 1947 to date. The library also has complete bound runs of the *North Carolina Anvil* and the *North Carolina Leader*, which are about five years old.

Duke University, Durham, NC 27706 has indexed the *Durham Morning Herald* and the *Durham Sun* from 1930 to the present.

NcHy

Elbert Ivey Memorial Library
420 Third Avenue, N. W.
Hickory, NC 28601

Indexed: Biographies, deaths, local news of historical import.

I: No charge, but there may be in the future.
C: $.10 per page, with $1.00 minimum.
ILL: Microfilm

NcMHi

Historical Foundation of the Reformed and
    Presbyterian Churches
Box 847
Montreat, NC 28757

Indexed: In addition to the *Asheville Times*, various and sundry
              newspapers in the United States, and some international periodicals, for any news relating to Presbyterian and Reformed Churches.
              Deaths, biographies, place names.
              Newsworthy events of the General Assembly, Synods, Presbyteries, and local churches; announcements about Presbyterians. In essence, anything concerning the Presbyterian and Reformed Churches.

I: No charge, but there may be in the future.
C: $.15
ILL: Some, on microfilm.

The Foundation is planning a cumulative index to the last 30 years of the quarterly newspaper, *Historical Foundation News*.

NcRGS   *

North Carolina Geneaological Society
P. O. Box 1492
Raleigh, NC 27602

Indexed: Marriages and deaths, together with all dates, place
               names, and other data related to each event.
*Marriage and Death Notices from Extant Asheville Newspapers,
1840–1870: An Index* compiled by Robert M. Topkins. $10.00
plus $.50 handling charge. Available from the North Carolina
Genealogical Society.

Although the book is labelled as an index, it is in reality an
abstract of newspaper records, as listed. The North Carolina
Genealogical Society does not have a staff to answer queries re-
garding specific information in the book.

All material for the book was obtained from microfilm of the
listed newspapers as filed at the North Carolina State Archives,
Raleigh, NC.

NcW

Wilmington Public Library
409 Market Street
Wilmington, NC 28401

Indexed: Marriage and death notices—not complete.
               Bound volume covering entire state is *Marriage and
Death Notices in the Raleigh Register and North Carolina State
Gazette, 1799–1893.*

I: No charge
C: $.10
ILL: Hard copies, $.25 each.

Marriage Contracts of New Hanover County Citizens, 1828–1855
(from deed books), covers New Hanover and surrounding counties.

NdMayS

Mayville State College Library
Mayville, ND 58257

Indexed: Clipping file.
Clippings are those which would be of interest in North Dakota history and those which preserve information about college events and graduates.

Deaths, biographies, place names, weddings, sports events, and anything that might be interesting about North Dakota and Mayville State College.

C: $.10

NdVcT

Valley City State College
Valley City, ND 58072

Indexed: Clipping file.
Mostly state subjects such as Garrison Diversion Project, and historical news; also some other general subjects such as child abuse, drugs, etc.

C: $.10
ILL: Microfilm

NhC   *

Concord Public Library
45 Green Street
Concord, NH 03301

Indexed: Selected clippings, and a limited newspaper index.
Scope of the index is mostly 1872–1920.
General subjects, including some deaths.

I: No charge. For detailed or prolonged search, inquire.
C: $.10 an exposure, plus mailing costs, when copying will
        not risk damage to the material.

NhCsM   *

Sandwich Historical Museum
Maple Street
Center Sandwich, NH 03227

Indexed: Clipping file.
            Deaths, births, marriages, biographies, events.

I: $4.00 an hour.
C: $.25

NhNa

Nashua Public Library
2 Court Street
Nashua, NH 03060

Indexed: Index cards, in file drawers.
            Retrospective indexing being done as time permits.
            All Nashua events, limited county and state news.
            No obituaries, except for very prominent persons.

I: No charge
C: $.10

NhPo   *

Portsmouth Public Library
8 Islington Street
Portsmouth, NH 03801

Indexed: Subject index, e.g. nuclear power plants, Portsmouth
            harbor development, coastal zone management.

I: No charge
C: $.15
ILL: Microfilm

NhR   *

New Hampshire Reference Room
Rochester Public Library
Box 1109
Rochester, NH 03867

Indexed: Indexing is just beginning. 1976 is the only completed
              year.
              All subject areas—vital statistics, education, religion,
government, health, politics, business, etc.

I: No charge
C: $.10 to $.15 per page, according to size.
ILL: Microfilm, 1864–1918. Hard copies not usually available.

NhS   *

Kelley Public Library
Main Street
Salem, NH 03079

Indexed: Important changes, new industries, celebrations,
              awards.

I: No charge
C: $.10
ILL: *Lawrence Evening Tribune* may be available from Law-
       rence, MA library.

NjCo

The Free Public Library
Haddon and Frazer Avenues
Collingswood, NJ 08108

Indexed: Clipping file.
Collingswood Library, Collingswood schools, Collingswood Commissioners and Commission meetings.
Some biographies.

The *Retrospect* is on microfilm, 1902–1971.

NjLi

Livingston Free Public Library
Memorial Park
Livingston, NJ 07039

Indexed: For *West Essex Tribune*—education, politics, elections, schools, library news, local organizations, township government, some biography, history. Card file.
For *New York Times*—news of current interest, statistics, government. Vertical file.

I: No charge
C: $.10

NjMhB

Burlington County Library
Woodlane Road
Mount Holly, NJ 08060

Indexed: *Mount Holly Herald*—marriages, 1837–1842; deaths, 1837–1842, January–June 1860. Will continue.

I: No charge
C: $.10 from paper; $.25 for microprint.

Burlington County Newspapers, $1.00.

NjMon

Montclair Public Library
50 South Fullerton Avenue
Montclair, NJ 07042

Indexed: 1961–1976 is complete; 1977 in process.
Montclair people, places, events of lasting interest.
Deaths, marriages, politics, schools, organizations,
etc.

I: No charge
C: $.10 per page, if lengthy reference.

NjNb

New Brunswick Public Library
60 Livingston Avenue
New Brunswick, NJ 08901

Indexed: Clipping file; very irregular.
Local news—city, county.
Deaths, biography, city government.

I: No charge; no extensive searching.

NjRw

The Ridgewood Library
125 North Maple Avenue
Ridgewood, NJ 07450

Indexed: 1976 in process; 1974 and 1975, clipping file.
News of towns of Haworth, Northvale (1974), Oak-
land, Oradell, Park Ridge, Washington Township, and Wyckoff
(1974 and 1975).
Local news, and state and nationwide news of area
interest.
Obituaries and local history.
Excluded are marriages and human interest stories.

I: No charge
C: $.10 or $.15

NjWhiM

New Jersey Room
Morris County Free Library
30 East Hanover
Whippany, NJ 07981

Indexed: All local news items.

I: No charge
C: $.10

1977 will be reproduced and available for sale—*Index to the Morris County Daily Record.*

Nm

New Mexico State Library
Southwest and Special Collections
P. O. Box 1629
Santa Fe, NM 87501

Indexed: Historical sites, legislative materials, Indians, biog-
              raphies, architecture, witchcraft, burros, crime, eco-
nomic conditions, other subjects related to New Mexico.

I: No charge
C: $.10
ILL: Microfilm and hard copies

New Mexico Newspapers, edited by Pearce Grove, $10.00. This is not a subject index, but gives the location of New Mexico newspapers throughout the state.

NmAl

Alamogordo Public Library
920 Oregon
Alamogordo, NM 88310

Indexed: Library news, weddings, obituaries, any sensational
news.

I: No charge
C: $.10 for Xerox; $.25 from reader-printer.
ILL: Microfilm

NmC

Carlsbad Public Library
Halagueno Park between Fox and Mermod
Carlsbad, NM 88220

Indexed: Biographies and historical articles on early Carlsbad.

I: Up to $2.30 an hour.
C: $.10

OCAJA

American Jewish Periodical Center
American Jewish Archives
3101 Clifton Avenue
Cincinnati, OH 45220

Indexed: A large range of contemporary and past American and
Western Hemisphere Jewish newspapers.
Anything dealing with Jewish life.

I: No charge
C: $.15
ILL: Microfilm

Jewish Newspapers and Periodicals on Microfilm, 1957, 1960. No price given.

OCHP

Cincinnati Historical Society
Eden Park
Cincinnati, OH 45202

Indexed: Local history—Cincinnati and Ohio.
Biographies and obituaries.

I: No charge
C: $2.50 service charge, plus $.20 a page.

OClPD   *

Plain Dealer Newspaper Library
1801 Superior Avenue
Cleveland, OH 44114

Indexed: All subjects.
Library also has *Index to Subject Authority Thesaurus,* January 1974 to the present.

I: Available only to newsmen. Public referred to Cleveland Public Library, Cleveland, OH 44114, which has essentially the same material.
C: Newspaper back issues kept for one month. Beyond a month, contact Microfilming Corporation of America, 21 Harristown Road, Glen Rock, NJ 07452.
ILL: No, but microfilm may be available through Western Reserve Historical Society or the Cleveland Library, in Cleveland.

OCoG

Reference Department
Grandview Heights Public Library

1685 West First Avenue
Columbus, OH 43212

Indexed: Clippings.
Biographies, place names, local history.
General subjects used by students, such as abortion,
firearms, capital punishment, diseases, death, etc.

I: No charge
C: $.10

Newspapers are kept only three months because of lack of space.

ODCL   *

Delaware County District Library
101 North Sandusky Street
Delaware, OH 43015

Indexed: Clipping file.
Biographies, local history.

I: No charge
C: $.15
ILL: Microfilm

ODa

Social Sciences Division
Dayton and Montgomery County Public Library
215 East Third Street
Dayton, OH 45402

Indexed: Newspapers have been clipped for approximately 40
years.
Material of historical importance is clipped.

I: Postage
C: $.10 for photocopy, up to legal-size; $.25 for letter-size
copy from microfilm.

ODaNR

Anne Hinton/North Research
Stillwater Pioneers
603 Rockford Avenue
Apartment 3
Dayton, OH 45405

Indexed: All names and places.

The Continental Correspondent was published near the Chesapeake Bay.

The *Stillwater Valley Advertiser* covers the Covington, Bradford, and West Milton trading zones.

I: SASE

Newspapers indexed are at the above address. *The Continental Correspondent* reprint by Fishergate, 2521 Riva Road, Annapolis, MD 21401.

OFph   *

Fairport Public Library
335 Vine Street
Fairport Harbor, OH 44077

Indexed: Clipping file.

Items of local history and about local people of interest.

C: $.10

OLeWHi

Warren County Historical Society Museum
105 South Broadway
Box 223
Lebanon, OH 45036

Indexed: Warren County biographies, obituaries, person interest stories, and articles of vital importance.

I: Donation fee at door.
C: $.25

SUMMARY OF WARREN COUNTY HISTORICAL SOCIETY
LIBRARY

690	general information files
879	family files
21	volumes of cemetery, marriage, and birth records
72,000	index cards on individuals
293	newspapers, 1807–1976
	court, census, and general microfilm rolls
67	bound copies of Ohio Historical Society quarterlies
1,030	catalogued volumes
	dozens of ledgers, diaries, and other interesting old books, magazines, and pamphlets

OLimaM   *

Elizabeth M. MacDonell Memorial Library
Allen County Museum
620 West Market Street
Lima, OH 45801

Indexed: Clipping file. Clipping has not been systematic.
Items pertaining to Allen County history.

I: No charge
C: $.10

OMenLHi   *

Lake County Historical Society
8095 Mentor Avenue
Mentor, OH 44060

Indexed: News items, obituaries, Lake County place names,
            local scrapbooks (clippings), local news, biographies,
etc.

Scrapbooks, containing hundreds of clippings, mostly
from the *Painesville Telegraph* and Cleveland newspapers, are
given every-name indexes. Other files are being collected daily
the past few years, not all into indexed volumes of clippings yet.
They include obituaries of war veterans, first generation Ameri-
cans' obituaries, golden wedding celebrations, and special articles
about the senior generation, prominent women, persons in the
performing arts, literature, music, sports, ships and shipping,
nursery and landscape firms, architecture, artists and sculptors,
etc.

I: No charge. SASE, plus duplication and postage.

ONorHT   *

Henry R. Timman
RFD #1 - Medusa Road
Norwalk, OH 44857

Indexed: Death notices and marriage notices.

I: $1.00 plus SASE.

$6.00 for abstract of papers, 1822–1835. 1835–1850 is not pub-
lished.

Newspapers are at Firelands Historical Society Museum, Norwalk, OH 44857.

OPaM   *

Morley Library
184 Phelps Street
Painesville, OH 44077

Indexed: Obituaries have been indexed from 1822–1932; and
              1935 to the present.
              Local news items have been indexed from 1971 to the
present.

I: No charge
C: $.50

OPosM

        Portsmouth Public Library
        1220 Gallia Street
        Portsmouth, OH 45662

Indexed: Deaths, biographies, local news items.

I: No charge, currently.
C: $.25

OWesaJG   *

        Mrs. Joe E. Gilbert
        Route #2, Box 399
        West Alexandria, OH 45381

Indexed: Mostly deaths.
              A few biographies, reunions, and probate notices
where the people lived out of the state.
              For pre-1850, there are references to deaths and
deaths outside the county.
              Mrs. Gilbert will be continuing to work on post-1907
indexing.

I: No charge
C: $.15

OkAr   *

Ardmore Public Library
Grand and E, N. W.
Ardmore, OK 73401

Indexed: Clipping file.
             Special events or local information, from *Daily Okla-
homan.*
             Local history in general—biographies, deaths, his-
tories, etc.
             From 1940's, some clippings of historical nature.

I: No charge
C: $.10, up to legal-size.

OkOk

General Reference Department
Oklahoma County Library
Northwest Third at Robinson Avenue
Oklahoma City, OK 73102

Indexed: Clipping file, arranged alphabetically by subject.
             Local and state affairs, including deaths, biographies,
and place names.

I: No charge
C: $.10
ILL: Microfilm

OkOkm   *

Okmulgee Public Library
218 South Okmulgee Avenue
Okmulgee, OK 74447

Indexed: Obituaries

I: No charge
C: $.20

OkTahN

Special Collections/Records Management Department
John Vaughan Library/Learning Resources Center
Northeastern Oklahoma State University
Tahlequah, OK 74464

Indexed: Clipping file.
            All dates are irregular.
            Northeastern Oklahoma State University, Cherokee
Indians, people of Tahlequah.
            Historical articles of Tahlequah, Cherokee Nation, and
surrounding areas.
            Obituaries.
            Political figures from local and state areas.

OrAst

Astoria Public Library
450 Tenth Street
Astoria, OR 97103

Indexed: Clippings indexed on cards; scrapbook format, made
            by City Hall staff.
            News of interest to city government—fires, accidents,
crimes, public relations, etc.
            Indexing on current *Daily Astorian* papers just
started.

I: No charge
C: $.10
ILL: Microfilm, from University of Oregon Newspaper Library,
        Eugene, OR 97403.

OrENC   *

Archives Department
Northwest Christian College

11th and Alder Streets
Eugene, OR 97401

Indexed: Clipping file.
            Deaths, marriages, athletic activities of Northwest
Christian College alumni, faculty, and students.

I: No staff to check for items; volunteer help only.

PCDHi

Library of the Delaware County Historical Society
Wolfgram Memorial Library
Widener College
Chester, PA 19013

Indexed: Deaths, biographies, items of historic interest.
            Delaware County Republican is indexed, and some
clipping has been done for the *Chester Times* and the *Delaware
County Times.*

I: No charge
C: $.25

PCarlH

Cumberland County Historical Society and
    the Hamilton Library Association
21 North Pitt Street
P. O. Box 626
Carlisle, PA 17013

Indexed: Marriages and deaths.

I: $5.00 research fee for checking family names, etc.
C: $.20

PGCoHi   *

Adams County Historical Society
Drawer A
Gettysburg, PA 17325

Indexed: Marriages and obituaries.

I: No charge, for one item.
C: $.20

PHan   *

Hanover Public Library
Library Place
Hanover, PA 17331

Indexed: Deaths, marriages, biographies, events, history.
              Buildings, organizations, local business and industry,
transportation.

I: No charge. Most requests are referred to the Hanover
      Area Historical Society, Hanover, PA 17331.
C: $.10

PLMHi

Lancaster Mennonite Conference Historical Society
2215 Mill Stream Road
Lancaster, PA 17602

Indexed: Mennonites, Amish, local history, obituaries, mar-
              riages.
              Intelligencer Journal—from 1900–1960, scattered clip-
pings of scattered issues.
              New Era—scattered issues.

C: $.25

PLig   *

Ligonier Valley Library
120 West Main Street
Ligonier, PA 15658

Indexed: Deaths, place names.

I: No charge
C: $.15 for Xerox; $.25 from microfilm.

PPFr

Friends Free Library
5418 Germantown Avenue
Philadelphia, PA 19144

Indexed: Clipping file of 250 volumes, known as the Irvin C.
Poley Theatre Collection. Card index.
Materials pertinent to theater productions in the area.
The years after about 1930 also include clippings of
motion picture productions.
Reviews, biographical sketches, obituaries, production
notes, etc.

I: $1.00
C: Varies

PPGHi   *

Germantown Historical Society Library
5208 Germantown Avenue
Germantown
Philadelphia, PA 19144

Indexed: Feature articles, subjects, biographical and genealogical.

I: $2.00
C: $.25 plus postage.

ILL: *Germantown Telegraph* and indexes are on microfilm and available through the Historical Society of Pennsylvania, 1300 Locust Street, Philadelphia, PA 19107

PPeSchw

Schwenkfelder Library
Pennsburg, PA 18073

Indexed: Marriages and deaths.

I: No charge
C: $.25

PR

Reference Department
Reading Public Library
Fifth and Franklin Streets
Reading, PA 19602

Indexed: Major events in Reading and Berks County. Some biographies.

I: $1.00 service fee.
C: $.25 per quarter of a page of newspaper.
ILL: Microfilm

PU

University of Pennsylvania Index
Reference Department
Van Pelt Library/CH
3420 Walnut Street
Philadelphia, PA 19104

Indexed: In general, all topics of interest to University community that will become University history.

Specifically, biographies, deaths, other personal name entries for faculty and student activities, names of campus buildings, names of student groups, specific continuing student activities, lecture series, individual speeches and speeches announced, dramatic and other presentations (individual or series) of individual schools of the University, pronouncements issued by administrative offices (Presidents, Provosts, Deans).

In-depth coverage, 1968 to the present.

Fair coverage, 1955–1958.

Slight coverage, from about 1898–1955.

Almanac, issued weekly during the school year, is the University's official publication of news of Faculty Senate, University Council, announcements from President's and Provost's offices, etc.

Pennsylvania Gazette is the monthly alumni magazine.

Library Chronicle is published by Friends of the Library of the University of Pennsylvania.

Pennsylvania Triangle is the magazine of undergraduates of College of Engineering and Applied Sciences and Fine Arts School.

Columns is an irregularly published student literary and topical magazine.

I: No charge, currently.
C: $4.00 minimum, plus mailing, for Xerox; $6.50 minimum, plus mailing, from microfilm.
ILL: Microfilm

PWcHi

Chester County Historical Society
225 North High Street
West Chester, PA 19380

Indexed: Somewhat spotty coverage. Only duplicate copies were clipped.
Deaths, marriages, topics of county interest.

RN

Newport Public Library
Box 8
Newport, RI 02840

Indexed: All local news—America's Cup, Tall Ships, council
meetings, etc.
Obituaries excluded.

I: No charge
C: $.10
ILL: Microfilm

ScCMu

Charleston Museum Library
121 Rutledge Avenue
Charleston, SC 29401

Indexed: No index—clippings.
Items concerning the Museum.

C: $.25

ScRhY   *

York County Library
325 South Oakland Avenue
Rock Hill, SC 29730

Indexed: South Carolina and local history and genealogy.
Pre-1940 years are intermittently indexed.

I: No charge
C: $.10

SdBro

Brookings Public Library
515 Third Street
Brookings, SD 57006

Indexed: Library maintains a pamphlet and clipping file for
Brookings and for South Dakota. These are small and
contain rather haphazard items of local interest.

I: No charge, but maximum staff time per inquiry is one
hour.
C: $.10

SdBroU   *

Reference Library
Library
South Dakota State University
Brookings, SD 57007

Indexed: Vertical file has some newspaper clippings.
Newspapers have not been clipped fully or consis-
tently over the years.
Local interest stories and South Dakota articles.

I: No charge
C: $1.50 for anything up to 15 pages, plus $.10 per page
thereafter.
ILL: Microfilm

SdWinT

Tripp County Library
Winner, SD 57580

Indexed: Tripp County history, homesteaders, place names.
School events, public notices, special events.
Organizations and officers, calendar of events.

C: $.15 for first 10 copies; $.10 per page thereafter.

TKL

Reference Department
(or McClung Historical and Genealogical Collection)
Knoxville/Knox County Public Library
500 West Church Avenue
Knoxville, TN 37902

Indexed: Some clippings go back to 1890's. More extensive
clipping began about 1960.
All subjects of local interest, including deaths, biographies, place names.

I: No charge
C: $.25

TNMPH

United Methodist Publishing House Library
201 Eighth Avenue, South
Nashville, TN 37202

Indexed: Library has clippings from all sorts of papers concerning various aspects of Methodism—history, obituaries,
etc.

C: $2.50 minimum.

TxAb

Abilene Public Library
202 Cedar Street
Abilene, TX 79601

Indexed: Deaths only, from 1975.
            Names and subjects in earlier indexes.

I: No charge
C: $.10
ILL: Microfilm

TxAm

Amarillo Public Library
P. O. Box 2171
Amarillo, TX 79105

Indexed: Abridged index covering the Panhandle area.
            Any materials of a historical nature, i.e. art, artists, authors, associations, biographies, business, college and universities, courts, crimes, departments of city government, drama, education and schools, foundations, obituaries, industry, etc.

I: No charge
C: $.25

TxGR

Archives Department
Rosenberg Library
2310 Sealy
Galveston, TX 77550

Indexed: All indexes are incomplete. The file is as complete as each current indexer wanted it to be.
            People, institutions, events, places, obituaries, etc.

I: No charge
C: $.25 per sheet: $1.00 minimum to mail copies from micro-
       film.

TxJaL

Henderson Library
Lon Morris College
Jacksonville, TX 75766

Indexed: Total paper microfilmed, with hard copy index.

I: Users may check free.

TxLMC   *

Ms. Marleta Childs
Box 606
Center, TX 75935

Indexed: Genealogical columns—"Kin Searching" in the Friday
             editions of *The Pioneer* and *The Times:* "Rootsearch-
ing" in the Wednesday edition of *The Times.*

I: No charge

Newspapers are in various libraries: Mahon Public Library, Lub-
bock, TX; Fannie Brown Booth Memorial Library, Center, TX;
and Special Collections, Stephen F. Austin State University Library, Nacogdoches, TX.

TxSaDR   *

Daughters of the Republic of Texas Library
   at the Alamo
P. O. Box 2599
San Antonio, TX 78299

Indexed: Staff clips all local news pertinent to San Antonio and
            Texas history, indexing according to subjects that per-
tain to Texas.
            Catalog has evolved through a period of time and is
unique, in that everything in the library relates to the history of
the area, from Spanish, Mexican, and the Republic of Texas
periods.

I: Materials must be used at the library. Material needed by
        historians and researchers is Xeroxed.
C: $.10 per page, letter-size; $.15 for legal-size; $.25 for
        document-size; within the state, add 5% sales tax.

A catalog of the library's holdings on maps, books, documents,
newspapers, photos, and clipping files (general only) should be
ready in early 1978.

                        TxW

            Special Collections Department
            Waco McLennan County Library
            1717 Austin Avenue
            Waco, TX 76701

Indexed: Clipping file.
            Buildings, historical sites and events, points of interest
in city, city departmental activities, organizational activities,
charities, hospitals, schools, etc.

I: No charge
C: $.10

                        UP

Vertical File—Young Adult Department
Provo Public Library
13 North 100 East
Provo, UT 84601

Indexed: Broad subject areas pertaining to Provo County and
the state of Utah.

I: No charge
C: $.05
ILL: Hard copies

USl

Salt Lake City Public Library
209 East 5th South
Salt Lake City, UT 84111

Indexed: Index is in the Periodicals Department; clippings are
in Special Collections.
Indexed—deaths, biographies, place names, local
news.
Clipped—local biographies, local place names, and
anything of local interest.

I: No charge
C: $.10 for photocopies of clippings; $.25 from microfilm.

Vi

Reference and Circulation Section
Virginia State Library
Richmond, VA 23219

Indexed: Marriages, deaths, biography, place names, houses,
events pertaining to Virginia.

I: No charge
C: $.10 per print, from reader-printer; $.15 per Xerox print;
plus $1.00 handling charge for each.
ILL: Microfilm, generally.

ViAl

Alexandria Library
717 Queen Street
Alexandria, VA 22314

Indexed: Vertical clipping file.
Material on Alexandria only—city departments, build-
ings, taxes, voting, etc.
Obituary notices only infrequently; historical data.

I: No charge
C: $.10
ILL: Only duplicate microfilm.

ViApCL   *

Appomattox County Library
Appomattox, VA 24522

Indexed: Clippings.
Deaths, biographies, special interest stories.

I: No charge
C: No photocopying service.
ILL: Hard copies

ViAr

Arlington County Department of Libraries
1015 North Quincy Street
Arlington, VA 22201

Indexed: Clippings are in Virginiana Collection and microfilm
reels are from Metropolitan Washington Council of
Governments.
Clippings in Virginiana Collection are on Arlington
County, regional area and state of Virginia. They cover biographies

(including obituaries), highway projects, transportation, politics, historical landmarks and events, government.

Microfilm reels in Reference Section include, for the metropolitan area (District of Columbia), clippings from area news-papers—environmental health, 1960–1971; health and welfare, 1962–1968; land, 1962–1970; public safety, 1962–1971; transportation, 1962–1971.

I: No charge
C: $.10

Library System Periodicals List, January 1977, $2.50.

ViPo

Portsmouth Public Library
601 Court Street
Portsmouth, VA 23704

Indexed: Vertical clipping file; filed under subject.
Clipping is fairly random and includes only selections.
Local interest material, local history, political biography, election results, campaign platforms.

C: $.10, up to legal-size.
ILL: Microfilm

ViRVB

Virginia Baptist Historical Society
Box 34
University of Richmond
Richmond, VA 23173

Indexed: Biographies, editorials, towns, educational institutions, personalities, churches—all relating to Virginia Baptists.

I: No charge

Newspapers are at the Virginia Baptist Historical Society Library.

VtA   *

Russell V'tiana Collection
M. Canfield Memorial Library
Arlington, VT 05250

Indexed: Indexed by subject.
              Deaths, biographies, events, industries.
              All items of major or historical interest regarding
Vermont, its people, places, etc.

I: No charge, but staff is limited.
C: $.10, at Town Clerk's office.

Library's file and clips are incidental to collecting V'tiana in all
forms—books, pamphlets, clips, etc.

VtSf   *

Springfield Town Library
43 Main Street
Springfield, VT 05156

Indexed: Clippings, in a local history pamphlet file.
              Clippings are mostly since 1930.
              Local events, some biography.

I: No charge
C: Through ILL, no charge up to 10 pages; $.10 a page for
        individual.
ILL: Copies

WKenHi

Kenosha County Historical Museum
6300 Third Avenue
Kenosha, WI 53140

Indexed: Deaths and biographies.

I: No charge
C: $.10

WLac

La Crosse Public Library
800 Main Street
La Crosse, WI 54601

Indexed: Biographies, with obituaries.
            Businesses.

I: No charge. Further research is $3.00 for the first half
      hour, $5.00 for every hour thereafter.
C: $.25

WMMus

Reference Library
Milwaukee Public Museum
800 West Wells Street
Milwaukee, WI 53233

Indexed: Clipping file.
            Articles about Milwaukee Public Museum.

I: No charge
C: $.20

WOshM   *

Oshkosh Public Museum
1331 Algoma Boulevard
Oshkosh, WI 54901

Indexed: Clipping file.
              Biographies, deaths, place names, Winnebago County
history.
              Steam boating on Lake Winnebago and Fox and Wolf
rivers.
              Menominee Indians, especially the Oshkosh family.

I: No charge
C: $.10

WRac

Racine Public Library
75 Seventh Street
Racine, WI 53403

Indexed: Clipping file.
              Biographies, local social agencies, city government,
clubs, schools, local businesses and industry, hospitals, local history, election results, celebrations, churches.

I: No charge for self-search; minimum fee of $1.50 for staff to
       check the file.
C: $.10
ILL: Microfilm and hard copies. Newspaper is discarded when
       microfilm is received.

WWeaJ

Janlen Enterprises
2236 South 77th Street
West Allis, WI 53219

Indexed: Jefferson County, 1853–1879—probate notices (all estates, guardianships, etc.).

Waukesha County, 1863–1881—marriages and
abstracts from obituaries (genealogical data only, not the long de-
scriptions, etc.).

I: $1.00 per surname, plus SASE.

Probate notices are in the Public Library, Jefferson, WI. Marriages and obituaries (from WPA project) are in the Waukesha
County Historical Museum, Waukesha, WI.

WWsPL   *

Marathon County Public Library
400 First Street
Wausau, WI 54401

Indexed: Deaths, biographies, place names, general historic
events.

Clubs, organizations, government and politics,
schools, business openings, churches, bankruptcies.

I: No charge
C: Probably $.10
ILL: Microfilm

WaSpHiE

Eastern Washington State Historical Society
Museum Library
West 2316 First Avenue
Spokane, WA 99204

Indexed: Clippings.

Other papers of the area are indexed when they are
available.

Biographies, place names, items pertaining to the Pacific Northwest and its history.

I: No charge
C: $.10

WvC

Reference Department
Kanawha County Public Library
123 Capitol Street
Charleston, WV 25301

Indexed: Clipping file.
West Virginia history in general—many subject headings.

I: No charge
C: $.10

WvMo

City-County Public Library
700 Fifth Street
Moundsville, WV 26041

Indexed: Local activities and organizations—aged, airports, animals, banks, Chamber of Commerce, churches, county government, elections and voting, etc.
Deaths and biographies are excluded.

I: No charge
C: $.15

WvSpCl   *

Roane County Library
Box 199
Spencer, WV 25276

Indexed: Local news items, feature stories.
               Times Record, from 1913–1975, is on microfilm.

I: $.50 to check through ILL, plus $.15 a page for photo-
        copies, or $.50 a page from microfilm.
C: See above
ILL: Microfilm

WvW

Ohio County Public Library
53 Sixteenth Street
Wheeling, WV 26003

Indexed: Indexing started about 1976. Other things have been
               indexed off and on since 1839.
               Local people, deaths, and biographies. Mostly Wheel-
ing items.

I: No charge
C: $.10
ILL: Microfilm

Library has a list of newspaper holdings.

WyCaC

Casper College Library
125 College Drive
Casper, WY 82601

Indexed: Clippings filed by subject headings.
              Before 1967, only occasional issues that have been do-
nated.
              Items having to do with Wyoming or history of the
West.
              Death notices.
              512 subject headings are used for material and some
will be divided.

I: No charge
C: $.10
ILL: Microfilm

WyEncM   *

Grand Encampment Museum
Box 395
Encampment, WY 82325

Indexed: A few other old newspapers of the area are also indexed.
             News of the Valley, especially mining news.

I: No charge
C: At cost

WyGrM   *

Sweetwater County Museum
P. O. Box 25
Green River, WY 82935

Indexed: Deaths, biographies, local significant items.

I: No charge
C: $.10

Guide to Wyoming Newspapers, 1867–1967, first edition, Lola
Homsher, Wyoming State Library, Cheyenne, WY 1971.

Materials are located in the Museum and serve the Sweetwater County Historical Society.

WyLarM   *

Laramie Plains Museum Assn., Inc.
603 Ivinson Avenue
Laramie, WY 82070

Indexed: Papers are not clipped. Research cards are used for
               biographies, deaths, history events, and pioneer
names.

I: $3.00 an hour, if staff member does the searching.
C: About $.50 per item, plus postage and handling.

WyShS

Kooi Library
Sheridan College
Sheridan, WY 82801

Indexed: Vertical clipping file.
               Local history, politics, business, educational material.

I: No charge
C: $.10